EUROPEAN CLOCKMAKING

THE HAMBURG
AMERICAN
CLOCK COMPANY

Published by

ANTIQUE CLOCKS PUBLISHING

1980 Edition 1000

Printed in the United States of America

ANTIQUE CLOCKS PUBLISHING
P.O.B. 21387
Concord, California 94521, USA.
COPYRIGHT © by Karl Kochmann 1980

*Library of Congress (USA) Catalog card Number
76-26338*

ISBN 0-933396-10-4

FOREWORD

Continuing my series on the technical and narrative history of European--
particularly German--clockmaking, THE HAMBURG AMERICAN CLOCK CO. (HAU) recounts
the origins and subsequent successes of the Landenbergers, a remarkable clockmaking
family from Schramberg in the Black Forest.

Much of my information came from personal interviews in 1977 with a few
old-timers and their relatives in Schramberg and with the late Dr. med. Fritz
Landenberger, at that time the last living son of Paul Landenberger, the founder
of the company. Data from the Historical Archive supplements that provided by
Dr. Landenberger.

A complete translation of THE FIFTIETH ANNIVERSARY OF THE HAMBURG AMERICAN
CLOCK CO., a booklet published in 1925, the year of the anniversary, also appears
in this volume. It relates the history of the company to that date, and once again
illustrates the fame, success, and first-class international reputation the HAU
Company enjoyed until its merger with Junghans A.G. in Schramberg.

As I have stated in previous works on industrialized clockmaking in the
Black Forest, my writings are intended to provide not only horologists and clockmakers, but clock collectors and those who are simply interested as well, with a
comprehensive and interesting history of the region, the founders, and the pioneer-
ing efforts involved in producing these clocks in what was often stormy and
difficult times.

In deference to a request by the late Dr. Landenberger, and for the benefit
of all those readers interested in the German language and culture (including
Switzerland and Austria), this book includes a section in German.

September 1980   KARL KOCHMANN
                                       Author and Private Publisher

1

INTRODUCTION
by
Herr Dr.med.

Fritz
LANDENBERGER
1978 +

Plate 1

During his visit, Herr Karl Kochmann asked me to write an introduction for his book, THE HAMBURG AMERICAN CLOCK CO.

The youngest of ten children, I am the last living witness to the past greatness of the accomplishments of my mother and father. My father began his career in 1868 as a manager with the Junghans Brothers Clockmaking Company, founded the same year. He quickly gained the confidence of Erhard Junghans, the cofounder. Erhard's brother, Xaver Junghans, after a short time with the company in Schramberg, returned to the United States, where he learned to make clocks using American methods. The two brothers did not get along very well.

Consequently, following Erhard Junghans' untimely death, my father was left in full charge of the Junghans Brothers Clockmaking Co. Although Erhard had two sons, both were unavailable to take over the business: young Erhard was in the military fighting the Franco-Prussian War, and Arthur was studying clockmaking in the United States. However, Junghans' widow, the owner and general manager of the business, restricted my father's chances for advancement, despite his marriage to her daughter Frieda (born 1851).

After lengthy unsuccessful negotiations, my father decided to utilize his knowledge of industrial clockmaking to start his own business. In 1875 the Landenberger and Lang Clock Factory was founded in Gottelbachtal. In 1883, for economic and financial reasons, my father changed the business to an open stock-holder corporation and changed the name to the Hamburg American Clock Factory, now located in Schramberg.

Using a production-line technique, their high quality clocks were successfully marketed worldwide. They used as a trademark crossed arrows ⨉ , and,
later, for the less-expensive selection, a small oil lamp . During their
peak production a work force of from 1500 to 2000 was on the payroll. A new section
of the city of Schramberg emerged around the factory complex.

In 1919 my father decided to retire in full health. He died on December 28,
1939, his birthday, at the age of 91.

Managemement of the factory then fell to his three sons, who had previously
been appointed company officers. In 1925 the company celebrated its fiftieth
anniversary with the slogan, "Where there is culture, there is an HAU clock."
After the anniversary my brothers and I considered a merger with Junghans
Brothers, which had also become a stockholder corporation.   1 3 170[*]

In 1932 the merger with Junghans took place, at which time the name Hamburg
American Clock Company disappeared. The merger proved to be an extremely painful
    2 3 170
event, especially for the Landenbergers, whose expectations were not met. During
his life, my father created a unique climate in the production facilities as a
result of his outstandingly humane and personalized approach. After the merger
in 1932, the former HAU employees deeply regretted the change because it brought
a depersonalized corporate atmosphere.   3 3 170

Herr Kochmann tells the story of the Hamburg American Clock Company and
their production of fine clocks. In so doing, he recaptures the past, prevent-
ing the HAU story from disappearing forever. I myself, at age 85 the last living
son of my parents, welcome this attempt from the bottom of my heart--contents
unknown--because I, like Herr Kochmann, wish that everyone might understand and
have a warm feeling for the past and the generations who were involved in it.

November 10, 1977
         Signed
         Dr. med. Fritz Landenberger

1 3 170* Refer to the footnote page(170)

"CITY HONORS SCHRAMBERG NATIVE OF POSTWAR TIME"

(Translated from the *Schramberger Zeitung* (Newspaper) of June 1, 1977)

Schramberg/Esslingen (West Germany)......

In connection with the 85th birthday of Dr. med. Fritz Landenberger, last Wednesday the city of Esslingen named one of her streets after this native son of Schramberg. In view of the outstanding achievements of Dr. Fritz Landenberger, the City Council voted a Landenberger Strasse to express their gratitude.

Fritz Landenberger, an opthomologist, was the American Occupation-appointed county supervisor for the county of Esslingen. Later Dr. Landenberger served as mayor of Esslingen until 1948.   **4 4 170**

In difficult times, Landenberger took over the crisis management of the city. Before the end of World War II, this private citizen approached the advancing U.S. Army to save the city of Esslingen from further bombing before the capitulation of Germany. On April 25 of that same year, Dr. Landenberger was appointed county supervisor, and subsequently became the mayor of the city of Esslingen. The 1948 election was won by the opposition candidate, Dr. Dieter Roser.

During his three decades as mayor, this 85-year-old did not avoid any political responsibility. His first priority was to deal with the shortage of housing and employment created by the influx of 20,000 refugees attracted by the nearly intact industrial community.

In addition to the burdens of administration, Landenberger found enough time to record and document the historical events of his time. His personal account of the Nazi regime and the postwar epoch are in the archives of the city of Esslingen. Of the few records available covering this period, Landenberger's are especially valuable because they enlighten the reader as to the political and sociological circumstances of that era. These invaluable records were used by Professor Borst in connection with the 120th anniversary of the city of Esslingen.

After 1948, Dr. Fritz Landenberger resumed his medical practice. For nearly half a century he was an active citizen of the city of Esslingen. After the death of his wife several years ago, Dr. Landenberger now lives a secluded life, but he is still an interested observer of Esslingen affairs.

For his birthday the City Council reached a unanimous decision to change

the name of the eastern part of the Eberhaldenstrasse in the Rubensteige to

Landenberger Street. This street parallels Muhlberger Street, named after Max

von Muhlberger, another mayor of Esslingen in the early 1900's who was dedicated

to the welfare of the city.

© by *Schramberger Zeitung*, vh.R4 R 1, No. 124.

◆ ◆ ◆ ◆

A MEMORANDUM

FROM: Dr. med. Fritz Landenberger 5 5 170
        Paracelsusstrasse 34
        7300 Esslingen a.N.

TO: The City Council
        City of Schramberg

Knowing my lively interest, my relatives in Schramberg have always kept

me up to date on matters reaching far beyond materialistic interests, and especially

on the activities of a group of people who are considering the formation of an

association for the "Endowment of Culture," sponsored primarily by Mr. Robert Nahr.

In the meantime, while these plans are perhaps taking shape, the 1967

Schramberg celebration should give many important reference points. I would like

to point out that the historical material stored in the city archives (temporarily

under the custody of Herrn Prof. Bopp) makes it possible--even more important for

future generations than the present--to examine reports on important events which

deal with the human shortcomings and weaknesses of the characters involved in those

events. The science of human behavior has explored the age-old question, *What is*

human?, in many ways, establishing the great importance of an archive like the one

in Schramberg.

I would like to point out to the members of the City Council of Schramberg

that the scholastic institutions do not have the only right to a place in our

society; we should also have a place where the young generations to come

can experience the past. In this connection I would like to draw attention to a

special matter very close to my own heart.

After the death of my father, Paul Landenberger Sr. (who was Honoured

Citizen in the city of Schramberg in 1928), the residence of my parents on the premises of the clock company had to be evacuated as a result of the merger with Junghans A.G. The children--eight of eleven were still alive at that time-- were interested in preserving the lifetime mementos of their beloved parents.

Nothing seemed more suitable than to preserve the location where my father had spent the last years of his life, the library, a room in which my mother had often spent many hours as well. The wall paneling and accoutrements were removed and stored in a nearby house, the so-called Garden Room section. The furniture, pictures, and personal mementos were from then on in the custody of Herrn Victor Luschka and myself. I took that opportunity to contact Herrn Mayor Dr. Hank and Herrn Prof. Bopp to create a memento room in the future museum in Schramberg.

The recreation of a Landenberger Room would bear witness to the personalities of middle class citizens instrumental in the clock industry in Schramberg in the last part of the beginning of the 20th century.

In 1972, after taking Mayor Dr. Hank and Professor Bopp to see the proposed memento room, I was assured:

> "The City Council has no objection to providing the requested memento room in the castle (museum), since you (Herr Dr. Fritz Landenberger) have declared your willingness to bear all the necessary expenses." 6 6 170

The city (Schramberg) assumed responsibility for transfering all accoutrements-- paneling, furniture, and so on--to storage under the jurisdiction of Oberbaurat (Chief City Engineer) Pitschak. This letter is intended--since Dr. Hank has been succeeded by Dr. Geitman as mayor and the City Council has also been restructured-- to recall a forgotten case at an opportune time.

I do not underestimate the problems involved in the realization of this project. I know the situation, especially considering the drastic structural changes that have taken place in the industrial sector, which are perhaps not temporary but a sign of our times. But the cultural life of Schramberg is too important. We must be willing to sacrifice a little for the cultural future. The museum is an important part of this future, so that young generations to come may draw upon our past as an enrichment to their education.

I will be most happy if the contents of this letter inspire Herrn Dr. Geitman and the City Council to a positive decision.

Respectfully,

Signed
Dr. med. Fritz Landenberger
May 1976

In Memoriam to Dr. Fritz Landenberger

FROM

The City of Esslingen a Neckar

In sympathy with the family we mourn the death of

Dr. med. Fritz Landenberger
Mayor (Retired)
Decorated with the Honor Plaque of the
City of Esslingen

During the surrender of the City to the American Army in April 1945, responsible for the distribution of essential goods in a time of deepest disarray and loss of the democratic system after World War II, outstanding credit is given this man for the establishment of the new   city of Esslingen. His labor on behalf of all was carried out with a high degree of responsibility, candor, and prudence. His work provided the cornerstone for the success and prosperity of our city in the last decades.

> In the name of the citizens, the City Council, and the Administration of the City of Esslingen a Neckar,

> *Signed*
> Erhard Klapproth
> Oberburgermeister

*All want peace, but not all are concerned
enough to lead to true peace.*
                                    Thomas A. Kempis

Esslingen
Paracelsusstrasse 34
April 1978

We mourn being parted from our uncle and greatuncle

Dr. med. Fritz Landenberger
opthomologist in Esslingen from 1927 to 1965
born May 25, 1892, in Schramberg
died April 5, 1978, in Esslingen.

We all miss him, he took full interest in our lives with love.

> In heartfelt, thankful remembrance,

> The Members of the Family Landenberger

Interment of the urn will take place in Schramberg.

7

CHAPTER II
INTRODUCTION to the fiftieth Anniversary
of the   HAMBURG-AMERICAN Clock Co.

THE FIFTIETH ANNIVERSARY OF THE HAMBURG AMERICAN CLOCK CO. *

Schramberg   **7 8 170**

One of the important lessons of the past, in the years during and immediately

after World War I, inflation introduced to the generation living today the knowledge

that the economy of a remote area can also be deeply affected by the principles of

capitalistic production methods. In an earlier day, social justice was a question

of the individual manufacturer, planning and making decisions on a product produced

by a working society in close involvement with the local economy, which was in turn

related to the national economy. Assessment of the future necessitates a look at

the past. The record of the development of the Hamburg American Clock Co. over the

last fifty years is filled with pride and success.

For the first ten years our company struggled to survive economically. The

latter years demonstrate that under extraordinary leadership the HAU company has

been able to accumulate fifty years of success and has deeply influenced the

economic and social structure of a large area of Schramberg and the surrounding

communities. The entire HAU is proud to be an integral part of the German economy

in the year 1925 and in the years to come.

* Abbreviated HAU

CHAPTER III

Paul Landenberger the Founder.

In 1869 Paul Landenberger aus Ebingen arrived in Schramberg at the age of 20. He could not then envision that this marked the beginning of very fateful years, that the little hamlet of Schramberg would encompass his future and his lifework-- the foundation of the Hamburg American Clock Co.

Paul Landenberger began his career as a clockmaker under Erhard Junghans Sr., founder of the Black Forest industrialized clockmaking industry, often called *the American System.* The untimely death of Erhard Junghans Sr. changed the destiny of Paul Landenberger, who was now appointed administrative assistant to the widow, Mrs. Junghans-Tobler. The limited opportunities within the Junghans company did not allow Landenberger to advance to a position consonant with his goals.

Paul Landenberger therefore decided in 1875 to establish with Herrn Phillip Lang the Landenberger and Lang Clock Factory, with a starting capital of 80.000 Mark (Goldmark). The times were not favorable for such an undertaking. The new industrial enterprise required all his energy and total dedication to build an efficient and well managed clock factory. But his efforts were highly rewarded, despite the hard times the HAU company experienced from time to time, interwoven as it was with the economic situation in Germany and worldwide.

Team spirit and the extraordinary efforts of his wife Frieda (né Junghans) helped to overcome these difficult times. The company was restless, driving forward with a large export market to Great Britain and her colonial territories as well as to Scandinavia. This effort provided enough hard cashflow, but not enough to increase working capital. The company was later changed to the Hamburg American Clock Co., a stockholder corporation. As such, the wellknown name was established worldwide by 1883.

Director and General Manager was Herr Paul Landenberger, assisted by Herrn Halbfass from Leipzig. The factory complex consisted of a main building and a few satellite buildings, with about seventy machines to produce the necessary parts and components. The payroll then included approximately 150 persons.

The stockholders' report in 1883 claimed with pride a very good market both domestically and for export. The fabrication program was enriched with a large selection of clocks. Constantly increasing sales required large expansions of the production facilities, so more land was purchased and their inventory of machinery was widely increased.

In 1887 Herr Adolf Halbfass resigned from the Board of Directors and Herr Christian Landenberger was appointed to fill his place. He first represented the HAU Company in London, then returned to Schramberg with the title of manager.

The years 1887-1880 exceeded sales from previous years by one third, and it was decided to enlarge the plant with new machinery. The annual report at that time stated:

> "The increased sales volume of this past year is primarily related
> not only to the price structure, but also to the quality of our
> product, making it unnecessary to lower the price merely to benefit
> sales volume."

The HAU Company tried to initiate an agreement of uniform price structure with other Black Forest clockmakers, but apparently it failed. Soon HAU had more than 300 on the payroll. At the world exhibitions in Melbourne, Australia, and in Hamburg, HAU received high awards.

To absorb the mounting costs of production and labor the management initiated a streamlined program to reward the members of the company with productivity bonuses, which in turn benefited the HAU Company by producing another sales record in fiscal year 1890-91.

New custom regulations were directed at the clock industry in the '90's, which resulted in a slight depressive impact. Finally the long-awaited connection between Schramberg and the European railroad network was completed. It is almost impossible to fully comprehend the methods by which all raw materials and finished products had been shipped previously, by horsewagon over lengthy steep mountain roads from Schramberg to the next existing railroad station.

The booming German economy again required expansion of the HAU operation. The payroll now exceeded 700 and a shortage of labor was experienced, requiring that a new facility be opened in Alpiersbach.   8 11 171

CHAPTER IV
The expansion of HAU.

In the last part of the nineteenth century many more expansions were undertaken. First a modern sawmill with a 400 HP power plant was erected. The factory complex previously leased in Alpiersbach was purchased outright for operation under the name Hamburg American Clock Factory — Alpiersbach in fiscal year 1900-01.

Unfortunately, the entire cabinet-clockcase plant was destroyed by a fire, but a new plant was soon built. A slightly reduced sales volume allowed the new cabinet-making facility to be rebuilt in a short time without any impact on production.

The stockholders decided to relocate the headquarters from Hamburg to Schramberg in 1900. When Schramberg was declared the new head office, further progress was made; but the shortage of skilled labor remained acute, so HAU embarked on a company-sponsored housing program to attract more skilled labor.

A hydro-electric plant was built and an Austrian branch was established in Bregenz in 1892. When large export contracts were disrupted by the war between Russia and Japan, the planned export quota was successfully shifted to other parts of the world.

Again, new customs laws with France forced the HAU Company to ship half-finished clock movements to France and a new assembly plant was shortly in operation near Paris (1905). By this time 1000 employees were on the payroll and the evermounting demand for clocks required expansion of the sawmill, the wood-storage, and the wood-curing facilities. Here a 325-diesel power plant was erected in 1910; in 1911-1912 the new casemaking facility was again enlarged to accomodate a wide selection of clock models of all types.

The following years were dominated by labor relations problems, taxes, and increased social programs. Absorbing these expenditures was out of the question, and increasing the retail price was not feasible. The HAU Company made every attempt to overcome these problems; 1300 employees were now on the payroll.

In 1914, within weeks after the outbreak of World War I, the HAU Company lost half their work force to the draft for the armed services. The situation was not the best for HAU in other ways as well. The company faced a drastic shortage of brass, copper, and high grade steel, all of which was now being diverted for defense purposes. Brass may have been replaced with steel, but the HAU Company always found a way to provide their customers with at least a minimum consumer product. The usual requisitions for war production did not stop the HAU Company; under most difficult circumstances, working both day and night shifts, the requisitions were filled to the best of their ability.

The end of World War I in 1919 was the signal for the HAU Company to shift again to peaceful production. Eighty-six company members did not return from World War I.

12

The adjustment to peacetime production, with severely limited materials and funds, was a tough challenge for the HAU management, but they met it with determination, considering the time and the circumstances. The burgeoning unrest of the labor force and the restrictions on the import of raw materials posed many problems for the head office.

Copper, brass, and all other metals were rationed by import quotas, which in turn required planning their distribution to all the clock manufacturers in the Black Forest area. Through concerted effort raw materials were purchased to sustain all the factories, whether large or small. The attempt to create a council to determine a uniform price structure, so as not to destroy each other by unhealthy competition, was at least partially successful.

Change in the political structure of Germany after World War I brought constantly difficult times, but good sense on the part of the management avoided any serious damage to the HAU Company. An effort to reopen their previous export channels was extremely successful, and the number one priority of the entire company structure was to streamline its operations.

The acute shortage of housing was met with an expansion of a housing project **9 13 171** in the Glasbachtal. In memory of the inflationary time, the main street was named Billion Street. In 1925 a condominium complex was erected. A good backlog of orders and the normalization of production were unfortunately overshadowed by raging inflation. The founder of the Hamburg American Clock Co., Herr Paul Landenberg, and his wife Frieda donated large sums of money for social welfare projects on the occasion of their fiftieth wedding anniversary. The most important event of those years took place when the factory was finally connected to a railspur.

The impact of inflation was so devastating there was no sensible relationship between production and real work. Often the HAU Company had to print their own money to meet the payroll when the bank did not have enough paper money on hand. Inflation undermined all incentive to increase production. In 1923 the German currency reform took place. Working half days was common in an effort to decrease the unemployment lines.

The fiftieth anniversary of the HAU Company opened with a balance statement in Goldmark. The annual report stated the true position of the company and anticipated a new and more prosperous future.

№37229 **GUTSCHEIN** *M. 50.000*

Die Gewerbebank Schramberg e. G. m. b. H. zahlt gegen
*diesen Gutschein im Verrechnungsweg oder wenn möglich
gegen bar an den Ueberbringer*

Fünfzigtausend Mark
Laufzeit dieses Gutscheines 4 Wochen ab Ausstellungsdatum.

Schramberg, den ....1 6. Aug. 1923....

Hamburg-Amerikanische Uhrenfabrik

INFLATION Money
Plate 2   Flaig archive

CHAPTER V
The management of HAU.

The HAU Company in 1925, their fiftieth anniversary year, enjoyed a top
position in the worldwide clockmaking trade. The HAU Company emphasized that
only with new and better production methods--the American System--could that
place be held in the years to come. The newest achievements in mass production
were introduced. Mass-produced latern gears of stamped brass replaced all other
methods. This American Method provided truly advanced mass production of good
quality uniform parts, service, and maintenance for the clock trade.

The HAU Company structure of an open stockholder corporation is a corporation
of a special kind. Most stocks are owned by the immediate family, close relatives,
friends, and acquaintances. This allowed an extremely stable stock situation,
with almost no sales or fast turnovers. This stability contributed immensely to
the solid financial structure of the HAU Company. The stock capital in 1925 was
3.000.000 new German Marks, with an additional 5.000 Marks in special stocks.

Let me now introduce the management of HAU.

PAUL LANDENBERGER, born 1848, was the founder of HAU, honoured citizen of the city of Schramberg, and a member of the Board of Directors. He retired in 1919. (See Plate 7 , page 49). His wife was Frieda Junghans-Tobler, born in 1851.

Both can look back upon a lifetime of work. They are the center of a large family, five daughters and five sons. The second son, Otto, did not return from World War I, but all the other sons worked for HAU. Two daughters, Mrs. Frieda Luschka and Mrs. Martha Gunsser, are very closely connected to HAU through marriage. Twenty-five grandchildren and six great-grandchildren look up to the parents with respect and promise to continue in the spirit of the founder.

WILHELM DEURER, Consul of Wurttemberg, was born in 1850. (See Plate 11 , page 53). Connected by a long friendship to the founder of HAU, he served as chairman of the Board of Directors after the company was changed from Landenberger and Lang to a stockholder corporation. His dedication and outstanding cooperation were of great service to HAU.

PAUL LANDENBERGER, JR., General Manager, was born in 1875. After beginning an apprenticeship in HAU, lengthy studies in Switzerland, England, and the United States enriched his education in business management. In 1900 he was promoted to comptroller of the company. In 1915 he became a member of the Board of Directors and from 1921 on served as General Manager of HAU. His personality determined the destiny of HAU. In 1918 he was elected Chairman of the Association of Clock Manufacturers within the economic council of the German clock industry. (See page 54 , Plate 12)

PAUL GUNSSER, Director, born 1869, joined HAU in 1895 and was promoted in 1897 to Administrative Manager, Financial Department. His territory included the procurement of all raw materials, as well as observing the proper usage of all materials purchased, and supervising the shipping department. He was named a director in 1921. (See page 55 Plate 13)

RICHARD LANDENBERGER, Director, born 1881, started as an apprentice with HAU in 1899. During 1901 and 1902 he served time in Paris as an apprentice to the HAU sales organization O. Carry. 1902-1903 he spent in London, returning to Paris in 1904. He returned to Schramberg for good in 1906. After 1911 he served as comptroller of HAU, becoming a Director in 1921. The estimating and payroll offices were under his direction, and he was in charge of the company-sponsored medical-plan insurance. He also participated in the sales department. His knowledge and his ability to parlay his technical and administrative skills to the benefit of the HAU Company made him an extremely valuable asset. Since 1922 he has been a member of the Black Forest Clock Manufacturers Association. (See page 56 , Plate 14)

KURT LANDENBERGER, Ing.Ph. and Technical Director, was born in 1878. From 1904 to 1905 he did research work in the United States on clock manufacturing methods. With HAU since 1905, he became an officer in 1912, and from 1921 on served as Technical Director.

FRANZ GOEDE, Comptroller, born 1866, started with HAU in 1896. After almost thirty years of service with the general accounting department, his expertise in the preparation of taxes and annual statements had proved his worth to the company. (See page 58 , Plate 16)

CHAPTER VI
HAU Production facilities.

The HAU production facilities occupy an area of 386.000 square meters (4,154,943 square feet). (See page 61 , Plate 17) In addition to the main complex, the company owns an alarm clock factory in Alpirsbach. More than 2200 persons on the payroll unite to produce the fine clock products distinguished by the crossed arrows and lamp of wisdom trademarks. An hydro-electric plant of 750 HP combines with two diesel power units of 775 HP each and a steam engine of

120 HP to provide all the energy for the plant facilities. Hundreds of machines of all kinds and applications stamp, roll, and machine the clock parts. The engineering department, with a staff of top engineers, technicians, and draftsmen, develops the clock models, working hand in hand with the tool and die section.

All precision fixtures are designed and manufactured within HAU's own facilities. The casings for alarm clocks are stamped in the HAU stamping plant. Clean large assembly-line facilities utilize as much daylight as possible to ensure a comfortable working climate for assembly of high-precision clock movements. Exceptional care is taken in the adjustment of timing in the calibrating section--no clock leaves the production line until it has been perfectly timed to high-grade standards.

The cabinet shop, which makes cases for the clocks, is a plant on its own merits. Selected lumber is cut in their own sawmill and dried in a modern curing facility. They give very special attention to all details of their wood treatment.

In addition to the social welfare system required by law, they maintain their own welfare system for white and blue collar workers, an indoor swimming pool, and other employee amenities.

Daily production of five thousand larger type movements (prorated to double that number of alarm clocks) amounts to a total production of fifteen thousand timepieces a day. This number is an average figure which includes the daily production of hall clocks, alarm clocks, mantle and wall clocks, and special clocks for industry, telephone companies, laboratories, and other technical applications.

In close cooperation with all dealers, the Hamburg American Clock Company constantly searches the domestic and world markets to discover the consumer's taste in style and type of clocks desired. Increasing promotion on the part of our dealerships is largely based on the superb technical quality and top workmanship of our production line.

The HAU trademarks, recognized worldwide, are:
The crossed arrows, which has been in use since 1891:
and the oil lamp (LUX), which has been in use since 1905:

CHAPTER VII
Outstanding employees.

Of the thousands employed by HAU over the years, several deserve special mention because of the length of their service and their devotion to the company. A total of 174 blue- and white-collar workers had more than 25 years of service with the HAU Company by 1925. From the records we have extracted information regarding specific individuals to add depth to our picture of the overall success of the company.

VIKTOR LUSCHKA (born 1858, died 1914) started with HAU in August 1891. Within a short time his spirit and his punctuality, his dedication and loyalty to the HAU Company had made him one of their most valuable employees. As a sales representative, he had an excellent relationship with their many customers and gained many friends for the company, especially in Austria, his primary territory, in which he was able to realize a high market potential for HAU. In 1911 Herr Luschka took an early retirement due to poor health. Before he passed away in January 1914, he had the great satisfaction of witnessing the beginnings of his son Victor Luschka Jr.'s career with HAU. For the past three years Victor Luschka Jr. has been in South America exploring the market for HAU. (See Plate 64 , page 20)

Others who achieved outstanding credentials with HAU include:

The Herren Daniel and Robert
FRIEDEL +

Between the years 1895-1903 the marketing and distributorship in Germany was notable expanded.

Herr Wilhelm Hecht+

Salesman during the years 1905-1915,remembered for his valuable contributions.Many of his friends remember his efforts.

Herr Paul Gunsser jun.+

The oldest son of Herrn Paul Gunsser,as or repres. in Hamburg and Hong Kong-there a deadly disease ended his very promising career.

Herr C.A.Hauser

From the year 1900-1910 Administrative and techn. manager.His expierency and knowlegde in the clock-watch trade contributed to the steady improvement of our products.

18

Herr Jakob Hauser+

General-Superintendent 1879-1915.For many years the manager of our tool and die shop,as well the entire technical machinery was under his supervision.

Herr Fridolin Lebmann+

Shop forman in the movement assembly shop 1877-1902.

Herr Erhard Günther+

Shop forman in the cabinet shop, 1880-1903

Herr Karl Simon+

Shop forman of the graphical shop 1886-1921

Herr Alexander Hilser+
1893-1924

Over 30 years ago startet as apprentice in the H.A.U.company,for two decades he was the superintendent of the clock production section.

CHAPTER VIII
Sales Organisation.

The salesorganisation and distribution of our products of the domestic and foreign market with wholesale outlets in the following parts of the world:

E U R O P E

```
Germany................Berlin,Bremen and Hamburg
Bulgaria...............Sofia
France.................Paris
Great Britain & Ireland.London
Yugoslavia.............Agram
Lithuania..............Riga
Poland.................Warsaw
Rumania................Bucharest
Spain..................Madrid
```

A F R I C A

```
Southafrica............Capetown,Johannesburg
```

A M E R I C A

```
United States of Northamerica: New York
Canada.................Toronto
Argentinia.............Buenos-Aires
Brasil.................Rio de Janeiro
Venecuela..............Caracas
```

19

A S I A

China..................Canton,Hongkong,Shanghai
                              & Tientsien
Japan...................Osaka
British India...........Madras & Bombay
Netherland India
(Dutch India)...........Amsterdam & Rotterdam

A U S T R A L I A incl.
N E W Z E E L A N D

Sydney

The HAU sales organization in Hamburg, Herrn Deurer & Kaufmann Co., should
be especially noted. The owners of this company were Herr Deurer, A. Lewerenz,
and A. Kaufmann, with Herr Deurer serving as the chairman of the board of directors. Connected to HAU since 1878, Herrn Deurer made outstanding contributions
to the organization. From 1919 on, Deurer & Kaufmann Co. represented HAU for
Chinese and Japanese export through the Import Bank Co., Hamburg.

CHRISTIAN LANDENBERGER, born 1859, began his career as an officer of HAU
in 1875 and assisted his brother Paul with dedication. He represented the company
in Paris until 1891, in Hamburg from 1883 to 1884, in London from 1884 to 1887,
and in Schramberg from 1887 to 1895. In 1895 he returned to London, but political
circumstances forced him to leave England in 1916, bringing him once again to
Schramberg.

His representation in London made an outstanding contribution to the
development of the company. After his initial return to Schramberg, he was succeeded by Herrn Th. Asher. The transfer had been set up in such a way that after
the death of Herrn Asher in 1895 the sales agency again reverted to the name
Landenberger Co. Landenberger's efforts resulted in the establishment of England,
with its colonial territories, as one of HAU's best export markets. After 1914,
the Combs Co. represented HAU in London. Combs had started his sales career with
HAU in 1887, in partnership with Herrn Hans Frutiger.

CHAPTER IX - The last fifty years of clockmaking.
This chapter treats the development
of the clock in the LAST FIFTY YEARS.

The history of timepieces reaches back for many thousands of years. Attempts to measure time, to record the high and low tides of the sea, to establish a fixed sequence for events can be related to the first traceable beginnings of our culture.

It should come as no surprise that from the beginning the requirement for perfect time measurement was the goal of several cultural epochs. While a sand-glass or sundial provided adequate measurement of time for earlier societies, our modern culture requires the services of the gear clock for better time measurement. During the time of slow transportation facilities, deviations in the timetable were tolerable; today the modern transportation system requires an extremely precise and dependable timepiece. Often the loss of seconds or minutes can endanger the life or safety of the traveler.

To understand the fast advancement in the importance of timekeepers, one must have a thorough knowledge of the development of the theory of timekeeping. We can assume the mechanical clock achieved its final design stage at the beginning of the 20th century. Of course, this does not mean the development of time-keepers came to an end--the electric clock, the wireless clock, and clocks related to radio technology give us many possibilities for the future. However, the mechanical problems of clocks have been solved.

For example, let us examine the alarm clock movement of the year 1875, confining ourselves only to the products of the Hamburg American Clock Co., which had just accomplished their extension to a large-size hall clock movement. Comparing this to a movement from the production line of 1925, we discover basic differences. The advancements of the last fifty years are displayed primarily in the gravity of the fabrication methods, rather than in the basic construction.

From the small beginnings of industrialized clockmaking during the 1870's, large factory complexes were erected. In the old days, daily production amounted to perhaps a dozen clocks; today thousands of clocks are produced daily, with the possibility for even further increasing production.

21

Expanded production facilities allowed the manufacturer to construct special machinery which could be operated by relatively medium-skilled labor, accomplishing in one step one part of the finished product. In the early days many steps were required, all performed by hand.

Expanded productivity also allowed a price structure that would attract a broad worldwide market.

Clockmakers have long held the opinion that the American System, with its stamped backplates, would not last long; but the quality work of HAU has proved the contrary. The precision tools and precision machinery of mass production guaranteed close tolerance. This was the primary advancement over the old days, when every part was handcrafted to fit and mesh.

The entire gearing of clocks was researched by these manufacturers; all modules were known. The form of the geartooth was essential; these inexpensive gears were all stamped gears. The friction between the gears was held to an allowable minimum, extending the lifetime of a movement. The construction of today's clock movements is precise, practical, and economical, promising a long life in usage.

Many movements, especially the more expensive ones, house their springs in spring barrels. The sheetmetal anchor of older days has been replaced with a Graham anchor. The selection of clock movements has also been expanded, with the rack strike system replacing the countwheel.

Immense improvements were made with the sound effect: the rod gong and spiral gong, the Westminster strike, and many other highly pleasing gong modulations enriched the strike effect, the melodic sound of the clock.

The cases of all clocks are related to the current styles in interior decorating, changing with the taste and style of the changing times. This is one reason the HAU Clock Company created more than 800 different styles for the worldwide market.

The Hamburg American Clock Company was determined to continue in the spirit of its founder, the production of high quality, tasteful, aesthetic clocks the goal of their concerted efforts.

EUROPÄISCHE INDUSTRIALISIERTE

UHREN HERSTELLUNG

HAMBURG AMERIKANISCHE
UHRENFABRIK

SCHRAMBERG SCHWARZWALD

im
SELBSTVERLAG
ANTIQUE CLOCKS PUBLISHING

Erste Auflage 1000

Gedruckt in den U S A

COPYRIGHT © *by Karl Kochmann 1980*
Katalog Karte Biblothek des Kongress U.S.A.
76-26338

ISBN 0-933396-10-4

VORWORT

Die historisch-geschichtlich-technische Abhandlung über
die "HAMBURG AMERIKANISCHE UHRENFABRIK "*ist eine Ver -
öffentlichung,die auf einen persönlichen Besuch des Authors
im Hause des Herrn Dr.med.Fritz Landenberger,dem letzten
lebenden Sohn des Gründers der HAU zurückführt.Das mir von
Herrn Dr.Landenberger und später von der Erbverwaltung zur
Verfügung gestellte Archiv Material und meine eigene
Sammlung gibt einen tiefen Einblick in eine ohne Beispiel
dastehende Pioniertat der "Landenbergers" in Schramberg,
Schwarzwald.Während meines Aufenthaltes in Schramberg im
Gasthof "Zum Paradies",dem Stammlokal der HAU Pioniere,
stellte ich fest,dass sich nur noch wenige Bewohner in
Schramberg sich an die Glanzzeit der HAU erinnern können.

Ich hoffe mit dieser zweisprachigen Veröffentlichung
im Sinne des Herrn Dr.med.Fritz Landenberger,und im Sinne
aller,die an der historischen Tradition des industriellen
Grossuhrmacher Handwerkes intressiert sind gehandelt zu
haben.

Die auf der nachfolgen Seite stehende Einleitung hat
Herr Dr.med.Fritz Landenberger noch kurz vor seinem Tode
im Jahre 1977,selbst verfasst.

KARL KOCHMANN
Author &
Selbstverleger

Concord,California
September 1980

Herr Karl Kochmann bat mich,eine Einleitung zu seinem
Büchlein über die"Hamburg-Amerikanische-Uhrenfabrik"in
Schramberg zu schreiben.Ich bin als jüngster Sohn meiner
Eltern-wir waren 10 Geschwister-noch der letzte Zeuge
unserer Generation,der einstigen Blüthe des Lebenswerks
meiner Eltern.

Mein Vater kam 1868 in die 1862 gegründete Firma
"Gebrüder Junghans" und erwarb sich rasch das Vertrauen
von Erhard Junghans (Sen.).Dessen Bruder Xaver kehrte
nach kurzem Aufenthalt in Schramberg wieder in die USA
zurück,wo er das amerikanische System,Uhrwerke zu bauen,
kennen gelernt hatte.Die beiden Brüder vertrugen sich
nicht so gut.-Als Erhard Junghans Anfang September all-
zufrüh für seine Familie und die Firma starb,waren beide
Söhne Erhard ju.und Arthur abwesend,der eine beim Militär
(Deutsch französischer Krieg 1870/71-der andere zum
Studium in den USA.So fiel meinem Vater die Leitung der
Fabrik,die im Besitze der Witwe kam allein zu,bis seine
Söhne zurückkehrten.Frau Junghans-Tobler verweigerte
meinem Vater den von ihm erwarteten beruflichen Aufstieg
in der Firma,trotzdem er seit August 1872 ihr Schwiegersohn war.Nach langen erfolglosen Verhandlungen entschloß
sich mein Vater,seine erworbenen Kenntnisse in der Uhrenfabrikation in einen eigenen Betrieb zu verwerten.

Im Frühjahr 1875 gründete er im Gottelbachtal die
Uhrenfabrik " LANDENBERGER & LANG ".Im Jahre 1883 wurde
sie aus wirtschaftlichen Gründen in eine Aktiengesell -
schaft umgewandelt unter den Namen
" HAMBURG AMERIKANISCHE UHRENFABRIK in SCHRAMBERG "
Die hier hergestellten Uhren fanden dank ihrer Qualität
auf einem grossen Teil des Weltmarktes guten Absatz.
Die Fabrikmarke zeigte ein Pfeilkreuz ✕ und später für
eine billigere Sorte eine kleine
                                  Öllampe.
In besonders günstigen Zeiten fanden 1500-2000 Arbeit-
nehmer ihren Lebensunterhalt und es entstand ein neuer
Stadtteil.

1919 zog sich mein Vater ins Privatleben zurück Kraft-
voll fast bis zu seinem Todestag,28.Dezember 1939,das
Kalenderdatum,das auch sein Geburtstag war,er war 91 Jahre
alt.-In der Direktion rückten 3 seiner schon lange in der
Firma beschäftigten Söhne auf,die,nach dem 50.jährigen
Geschäftsjubiläum 1925 die Fusion mit der Firma Gebrüder
Junghans,unterdessen auch eine A.G.und von ihren Vettern
Junghans geleitet,ins Auge fassten.In der Festschrift
hiess es damals:" WO EINE SPUR VON KULTUR FINDET MAN DIE
PFEILKREUZUHR "

Die Fusion kam zustande und 1932 verschwand schliesslich
der Firmen Name " HAMBURG - AMERIKANISCHE UHRENFABRIK "
des kleinen Partners. 2 25 172*

Ein ausserordentlich schmerzliches Ereignis,um so mehr
als sich die Erwartungen,die man von unserer Seite an die
Fusion geknüpft hatten,nicht erfüllten,und der Geist meines
Vaters der der Atmosphäre in der Fabrik einen besonderen
menschlichen Character bis zuletzt verliehen hatte,zum
Leidwesen der treuen Beamten u.Arbeiter,einer unpersön -
lichen Arbeit wich. 3 25 172

Herr Kochmann lässt mit diesen Büchlein die " HAMBURG
AMERIKANISCHE UHRENFABRIK " und ihre Erzeugnisse noch
einmal auferstehen und entreißt sie damit der Vergessenheit.

Dass ich,der letzte noch lebende Sohn (85)meiner
Eltern diese Absicht von Herzen begrüsse,wiewohl ich seinen
Inhalt noch nicht kenne,wird jeder verstehen,der wie Herr
Karl Kochmann,ein warmes Gefühl für die Vergangenheit,für
die vorausgegangenen Generationen hat.

                              Unterzeichnet:

                              Dr.med.Fritz Landenberger

*Fußnote Hinweis
 172= Seitenzahl

Anmerkung des Authors:

*Das von Herrn Dr.Fritz Landenberger
verfasste Schreiben wurde im Inhalt
und der Satzstellung unverändert im
Schreibmaschinen Text gehalten.*

Einleitung (Vorwort)

Herr Karl Kochmann bat mich, eine Einleitung 10.11.77 zu seinem Büchlein über die „Hamburg-Amerikanische Uhrenfabrik in Schramberg" zu schreiben. Ich bin als jüngster Sohn meiner Eltern — Wir waren 10 Geschwister — noch der letzte Zeuge unserer Generation der einstigen Blüthe des Lebenswerks meiner Eltern.

Mein Vater kam 1868 in die 1862 gegründete Firma „Gebrüder Junghans" & erwarb sich rasch das Vertrauen von Erhard Junghans. Dessen Bruder Xaver kehrte nach kurzem Aufenthalt in Schramberg wieder in die U.S.A. zurück, wo er das amerikanische System, Uhrwerke zu bauen, kennen gelernt hatte. Die beiden Brüder vertrugen sich nicht so gut. — Als Erhard Junghans Anfang September allzu früh für seine Familie & die Firma starb, waren seine Söhne Erhard & Arthur abwesend, der eine beim Militär (deutsch-französischer Krieg 1870/71), der andere zum Studium in den U.S.A. So fiel meinem Vater die Leitung der Fabrik, die in dem Besitz der Frau Erhard Kaw Jun. alleine zu, bis die Söhne zurückkehrten. Frau Junghans - Tobler verweigerte meinem Vater den von ihm erwarteten beruflichen Aufstieg in der Firma, trotzdem er seit August 1872 ihr Schwiegersohn war. Nach langen erfolglosen Verhandlungen entschloss sich mein Vater, seine erworbenen Kenntnisse in der Uhrenfabrikation in einem eigenen Betrieb zu verwirklichen. Im Jahre 1875 gründete er im Göttelbachtal die Uhrenfabrik „Landenberger & Lang". Im Jahre 1883 wurde sie aus wirtschaftlichen Gründen in eine Aktiengesellschaft umgewandelt unter dem Namen „Hamburg-Amerikanische Uhrenfabrik in Schramberg". Die in ihr hergestellten Uhren fanden denk

ihrer Qualität auf einem grossen Teil des Weltmarkts (2)
guten Absatz. Die Fabrikmarke zeigte ein Pfeilkreuz
u. Spott für eine billigere Sorte eine kleine Öllampe.
In den besonders Zeiten fanden 1500 – 2000 Arbeitnehmer
ihren Lebensunterhalt u. es entstand ein neuer Stadtteil.

1919 zog sich mein Vater ins Privatleben zurück
Kraftvoll fest bis zu seinem Todestag 28. Dezember 1939,
das Kalenderdatum, das auch das seines Geburtstags war
Er war 91 Jahre alt. – In die Direktion rückten 3 seiner
schon lange in der Firma beschäftigten Söhne auf, die, nach
dem 50jährigen Geschäftsjubiläum 1925 die Fusion mit
der Firma Gebrüder Junghans, unterdessen auch eine A.G., in der Festschrift lieser
stabten. u. von den Vetter Junghans, ins Auge fassten. Die damals: Wo einer Herr nur von Weltburg
Fusion Kunstschule u. 1932 schwand schliesslich der Firma Sicht man die Pfeilkreuzfabrik
Name „Hamburg-Amerikanische Uhrenfabrik", des kleineren Partners.
ein ausserordentlich schmerzliches Ereignis, um so mehr als
die Erwartungen, die man von unserer Seite an die Fusion geknüpft hatte, nicht erfüllten, a der Geist meines Vaters
der der Atmosphäre in der Fabrik einen besonders menschlichen Charakter bis zuletzt verlieh, Zum Leidwesen der neuen
Beamten u. Arbeiter eine unpersönliche Zusammenarbeit will.

Herr Kochmann lässt mit diesem Büchlein die
„Hamburg-Amerikanische Uhrenfabrik" u. ihre Erzeugnisse
noch einmal auferstehen u. entreisst sie damit der Vergessenheit. Dass ich, der letzte noch lebende Sohn (85)
meiner Eltern dies Absicht von Herzen begrüsse, wiewohl ich
seinen Inhalt noch nicht kenne, wird jeder verstehen, der
wie Herr Kochmann, ein warmes Gefühl für die Vergangenheit
für die vorausgegangenen Generationen hat

Dr. med. Fritz Lembergere

27

Memorandum   5 28 172

Mit lebhaftem Interesse verfolge ich – durch Verwandte in Schramberg
jeweils darüber unterrichtet – die über materielle Interessen hinausgehenden
Bestrebungen, einen "Förderverein Kulturhaus" zu gründen, hervorgegangen
aus den Anregungen des Gewerbevereinsvorsitzenden, Herrn Robert Nähr.
Ja, unterdessen ist er vielleicht schon verwirklicht, die Feier des Stadt-
jubiläums 1967 bietet ihm wohl mancherlei Anhaltspunkte. Ich darf hier vor
allem auf das hinweisen, was im städtischen Archiv an Erinnerungen und
Schilderungen aus vergangener Zeit, möglichst griffbereit, aufbewahrt wird
(zur Zeit unter der Obhut von Herrn Professor Bopp) und, wahrscheinlich
mehr als im Augenblick, der jetzigen und jeder kommenden Generation Wich-
tiges erzählen kann: über menschliche Schwächen und über bewährte Charak-
tere im Blick auf bedeutsame Ereignisse. – Die Wissenschaft der Psychologie
hat vieles im Verhalten der Menschen aufgeklärt, aber wohl noch tiefer be-
antwortet die Geschichte die alte Frage: Was ist der Mensch? – Drum ist ein
Archiv, auch das in Schramberg, von so grosser Bedeutung. Darf man hier
die Mitglieder des Gemeinderats darauf aufmerksam machen, dass auch
diese Institution, nicht weniger als die Schule mit der heranwachsenden Generation, ein Recht auf Räume hat, die der von ihr geleisteten Arbeit Genüge
tut. – Ich möchte aber in diesem Zusammenhang auf etwas Weiteres Ihre
Aufmerksamkeit lenken, das, wie Sie begreifen werden, mir besonders am
Herzen liegt.

Nach dem Tod meines Vaters, Paul Landenberger dem Älteren (1928 zum
Ehrenbürger der Stadt Schramberg ernannt) musste, durch die Ungunst der
seinerzeitigen Fusionsabmachungen zwischen der Hamburg-Amerikanischen
Uhrenfabrik und der Firma Gebrüder Junghans A.G. bedingt, das Wohnhaus
der Eltern geräumt werden. Ihre Kinder, acht von elfen lebten noch, hatten
das Bedürfnis, ihrer Eltern mit einem langen Leben gesegnete Lebensart in
der Erinnerung festzuhalten. Nichts schien dazu geeigneter als das Zimmer
zu erhalten, in dem mein Vater seine letzten Jahre in erster Linie verbrachte
(Bibliothek genannt), und in dem auch meine Mutter oft und oft bei ihm ver-
weilte. – So wurde es, mit allem Drum und Dran, den Wandverkleidungen, den
Schränken und Schreibtischen und Bildern etc. in den dem Wohnhaus gegenüber-
liegenden sogenannten Gartensaalbau verlegt, wo es bis vor wenigen Jahren
unter den Augen von Herrn Viktor Luschka, auch meiner Pflege unterlag.
Da kündigte die Firma Junghans den Raum. – Ich nahm deshalb Gelegenheit,
mich mit Herrn Oberbürgermeister Dr. Hank und Herrn Professor Bopp in
Verbindung zu setzen, denn von Anfang an war das Gedächtniszimmer einem
künftigen Heimatmuseum zugedacht. Repräsentiert es doch die Zeit und Per-
sönlichkeiten, denen die Entwicklung der Uhrenindustrie in Schramberg im

English transl.see page 5

28

letzten Drittel des vorigen und zu Beginn des 20. Jahrhunderts zu verdanken
war: Das gehobene Bürgertum. - Im Jahre 1972 erhielt ich, nach einer Be-
sichtigung des Gedächtniszimmers und einer Rücksprache mit Herrn Oberbürgermeister Dr. Hank und Herrn Professor Bopp die Versicherung:

"Der Gemeinderat ist grundsätzlich bereit, im Schloss das von Ihnen
gewünschte Gedächtniszimmer einzurichten, nachdem Sie sich zur
Übernahme der Kosten bereiterklärt haben."

Die Stadt hat dann das Zimmer durch Herrn Oberbaurat Pitschak übernommen
und eingelagert.

Diese Zeilen haben nun die Absicht, nachdem in Schramberg ein neuer Oberbürgermeister, Herr Dr. Geitmann, an die Stelle von Herrn Dr. Hank getreten ist, und wohl auch der Gemeinderat unterdessen einige neue Köpfe erhielt, an etwas zu erinnern, was im Lauf der Zeit natürlicherweise in den
Hintergrund getreten ist. Ich verhehle mir die Schwierigkeiten nicht, die die
Gemeindeverwaltung und der Gemeinderat zur Realisierung des oben erwähnten
Planes zu überwinden hat. Ich kenne die pekuniären Hemmungen, die zur Zeit
keinem Gemeindewesen erspart sind, und die letzten Endes mit den Veränderungen
in der Industrie zusammenhängen, und die wahrscheinlich nicht vorübergehend
sein werden. Um so mehr dürfte für Schrambergs Zukunft das kulturelle Leben
von Bedeutung sein, das für manchen materiellen Verzicht eine geistige Bereicherung verspricht. Dazu wird ein Heimatmuseum Wesentliches beitragen
können und, wohlgemerkt! auch die heranwachsende Jugend wird von diesem
vielseitigen Erziehungsmittel grossen und dauernden Vorteil haben.

Es würde mich freuen, wenn ich mit meinen Ausführungen den Herrn Oberbürgermeister Dr. Geitmann und die Mitglieder des Gemeinderats zu positiven
Überlegungen veranlassen könnte.

Hochachtungsvoll

(Dr. Fritz Landenberger)

English transl.see page 6

Mittwoch, 1. Juni 1977

Verdienste in der Nachkriegszeit
Landenbergerstraße in Esslingen

Stadt würdigt gebürtigen Schramberger / Verdienste in der Nachkriegszeit

vh. **Schramberg/Esslingen.** Anläßlich des 85. Geburtstages von Dr. Fritz Landenberger am Mittwoch letzter Woche hat die Stadt Esslingen eine Straße nach dem gebürtigen Schramberger benannt. Wie dazu von der Stadtverwaltung Esslingen zu erfahren war, wählte der Gemeinderat diese Geste, um ihm für seine in der Nachkriegszeit erworbenen Verdienste für die Stadt zu danken. Fritz Landenberger — von Beruf Augenarzt — wurde nach dem zweiten Weltkrieg von der amerikanischen Militärregierung zuerst als Landrat des Kreises Esslingen und dann auch als Oberbürgermeister der Stadt Esslingen eingesetzt. Das Amt des Oberbürgermeisters führte er bis 1948.

In schwieriger Zeit hatte Landenberger das erste Krisenmanagement für die Stadt übernommen. Vor Ende des Krieges und der Stadtübergabe war er damals noch als Privatmann den amerikanischen Militärs entgegengeeilt, um die Stadt vor der drohenden Bombardierung zu retten. Von der Militärregierung wurde er am 25. April 1945 als Landrat eingesetzt. Am 1. September 1945 wurde er auch als Oberbürgermeister von Esslingen eingesetzt. Er führte ein Doppelamt bis im Juli 1946 Georg Geist als Landrat gewählt wurde. Im Monat davor war Landenberger vom Gemeinderat der Stadt Esslingen als Oberbürgermeister gewählt worden. Bei der nächsten Wahl 1948 unterlag er seinem Gegenkandidaten Dr. Dieter Roser.

In den rund drei Jahren seiner OB-Zeit hatte sich der heute 85jährige nicht gescheut, politische Verantwortung zu übernehmen. Das hieß damals: Wohnungsnot lindern, Arbeitsplätze beschaffen, die erste Versorgung der Bevölkerung gewährleisten in einer Stadt, die ungeheuer angewachsen war durch einen Zustrom von rund 20 000 Flüchtlingen, die durch die dortige Industrie angelockt wurden.

Neben den Entscheidungen, die er zu treffen hatte, nahm sich Landenberger Zeit für eine Dokumentation der Geschehnisse. Seine persönlichen Schriften aus dem unmittelbaren Erleben des Naziregimes und der Nachkriegszeit dienen heute der wissenschaftlichen Auswertung für das Stadtarchiv. „Von dem Wenigen schon zum Besten gehören seine Aufzeichnungen über die Ereignisse", wie es dazu von der Stadtverwaltung heißt. Landenberger diene als anerkannter Lieferant für das Stadtarchiv. Er bringe Licht in die Vorgänge, die Professor Borst im Zusammenhang mit der 120-Jahr-Feier in diesem Jahr recherchiere und zusammenstelle.

Nach 1948 eröffnete Dr. Landenberger wieder eine Augenarztpraxis Nahezu ein halbes Jahrhundert ist er inzwischen Bürger dieser Stadt. Er lebt zurückgezogen nach dem Tode seiner Frau vor wenigen Jahren, gehört aber weiter zu den aufmerksamen Beobachtern der Vorgänge in Esslingen.

Zu seinem Geburtstag wurde der östliche Teil der Ebershaldenstraße und die Rübgartensteige auf einmütigen Beschluß des Gemeinderats in Landenberger Straße umbenannt. Der Straßenzug verläuft im übrigen parallel zur Mühlberger Straße, so benannt nach dem Bürgermeister Max von Mühlberger, der sich in den ersten Jahrzehnten des Jahrhunderts für Esslingen verdient gemacht hat.

6 30 172

English transl. see page 4

30

Frieden wollen alle haben,
aber nicht alle sind besorgt für das,
was zum wahren Frieden führt.
Thomas A. Kempis

Esslingen, Paracelsusstraße 34
im April 1978

Wir haben Abschied genommen von unserem Onkel und
Großonkel

Dr. med. Fritz Landenberger

von 1927 bis 1965 Augenarzt in Esslingen

geboren am 25. Mai 1892 in Schramberg
gestorben am 5. April 1978 in Esslingen

Wir werden ihn vermissen, denn er hat unser Leben in
liebevollster Anteilnahme begleitet.

In herzlichem, dankbarem Gedenken

Die Nachkommen
der Familie Landenberger

Die Beisetzung der Urne erfolgt in Schramberg

STADT ESSLINGEN AM NECKAR

In Trauer und Verbundenheit mit den Angehörigen beklagen wir den Tod von

Dr. med. Fritz Landenberger

Oberbürgermeister a. D.
Träger der Ehrenplakette der Stadt Esslingen am Neckar

Bei der Übergabe der Stadt an die amerikanischen Streitkräfte im April 1945, bei der Versorgung der Bürgerschaft mit den Gütern des notwendigsten Lebensbedarfs in Zeiten existentieller Not und nicht zuletzt bei der Wiederherstellung demokratischer Verhältnisse nach dem 2. Weltkrieg, hat er sich um die Stadt Esslingen am Neckar bleibende Verdienste erworben.

Seine Arbeit für die Allgemeinheit war getragen von hoher Verantwortung, von Sachlichkeit, Freimut und Offenheit. Durch sein Wirken hat der Verstorbene den Grundstein für das Wachstum und Gedeihen unserer Stadt in den letzten Jahrzehnten gelegt.

Im Namen der Bürgerschaft, des Gemeinderates und der
Verwaltung der Stadt Esslingen am Neckar

Eberhard Klapproth
Oberbürgermeister

English transl. see page 7

31

CHAPTER XI

Denkschrift 7 32 172

zum 5ojährigen Bestehen

der

Hamburg-Amerikanischen
Uhrenfabrik

in

Schramberg

(Württemberg)

1 · 9 · 2 · 5

= NACHDRUCK =

SCHRAMBERG
die Heimat der Hamburg-Amerikanischen Uhrenfabrik (H.A.U.)

Plate 2
Artist conception of the
Hamburg-American Clock Company (H.A.U.)
Artist,R.Nägele

10 33 172

33

ERST die Erfahrungen des letzten Jahrzehnts, die Jahre des Krieges und die Zeiten der Währungszerrüttung haben den heute lebenden Generationen die Bedeutung der Zusammenhänge ganz klar gemacht, in die sie mit ihrer Arbeit tätig eingegliedert sind: die Weltwirtschaft im allgemeinen und das deutsche Wirtschaftsleben im besonderen. Dabei ist uns zum Bewußtsein gekommen, wieviel Problematisches in diesem vorher anscheinend so sicher und selbstverständlich arbeitenden Organismus des auf kapitalistischer Grundlage aufgebauten Produktionsprozesses noch enthalten ist. Früher schien allein der soziale Ausgleich die brennende Frage des Tages zu sein, und gewiß müssen die Bemühungen um ihre befriedigende Beantwortung ungemindert weitergehen, aber anders als je bisher reckt sich heute über alle Schwierigkeiten der Wirtschaft drohend die Gefahr auf, daß der Produktionsprozeß, der der Mehrzahl des deutschen Volkes die Lebensfristung ermöglicht, der unserm gesamten öffentlichen und gesellschaftlichen Leben seinen Stempel aufdrückt, infolge gewollter und ungewollter Störung der weltwirtschaftlichen Zusammenhänge zum Stillstand kommt. Die Folgen eines solchen Ereignisses wären unabsehbar!

7

❡ Dieser Ausblick in eine ernste Zukunft gibt unserer Festschrift, die einem Gedenktag der Arbeit ihr Entstehen verdankt, eine über die Rückschau hinausgehende Aufgabe. Wenn uns die Entwicklung der Hamburg-Amerikanischen Uhrenfabrik in den letzten 50 Jahren mit Stolz erfüllen darf, so wollen wir um so mehr ohne jede Selbsttäuschung die Zukunft betrachten. Wie das erste Jahrzehnt des Bestehens unseres Unternehmens an Schwierigkeiten reich war, so scheint auch der Beginn der zweiten Jahrhunderthälfte besondere Umsicht und Anstrengungen in der Leitung zu verlangen.

❡ Mögen unsere Freunde aus der Geschichte der Hamburg-Amerikanischen Uhrenfabrik in den ersten 50 Jahren ihres Bestehens, die wir hier vorlegen, die Überzeugung gewinnen, daß das Unternehmen in einem Geiste geleitet wurde und geleitet wird, der sich immer der Bedingtheit erfolgreicher Arbeit durch das große Ganze bewußt ist und der zu seinem Teil an der Wohlfahrt unseres ganzen Volkes mitarbeiten will.

8

Fabrikansicht vom Jahre 1875

ALS junger Kaufmann im Alter von wenig mehr als 20 Jahren kam Paul Landenberger aus Ebingen im Frühjahr 1869 nach Schramberg. Er ahnte damals nicht, daß ihm die kleine Schwarzwaldstadt nicht nur zum künftigen dauernden Aufenthalt bestimmt war, sondern daß er hier auch den Grund legen werde zu seinem Lebenswerk, das heute als die Hamburg-Amerikanische Uhrenfabrik vor uns steht.

◖ Paul Landenberger begann seine Tätigkeit in der Fabrik von Erhard Junghans dem Älteren, dem Begründer der Uhrenindustrie im Schwarzwald nach dem sogenannten amerikanischen System. Da er nach dessen Tod in diesem Unternehmen für sich nicht die gewünschten Entwicklungs-

9

Plate 3
Factory complex,year 1876-1884   8 36 172

möglichkeiten fand, gründete er im Jahre 1875, zusammen mit Herrn Philipp Lang aus St. Johann, eine eigene Großuhrenfabrik unter der Firma „Landenberger & Lang". Mit einem Kapital von 80000 Mark wurde die Arbeit begonnen.

❡ Es war damals keine günstige Zeit für die Gründung von Industrieunternehmungen, und so bedurfte es aller Energie und unermüdlicher Arbeit, um die Aufnahme einer regelmäßigen Uhrenfabrikation zu erreichen. Die Mühe wurde belohnt, — aber die Zeiten, in welche die Kinderjahre des Unternehmens fielen, blieben hart; sie sind ja in der Wirtschaftsgeschichte Deutschlands als besonders kritische bekannt. So mußte auch das junge Unternehmen, trotz aller Tatkraft seines Leiters, dem in seiner Gattin Frida, einer Tochter von Erhard Junghans, eine treue Mitarbeiterin zur Seite stand, die schwersten Stürme durchmachen. Wohl gelang es, mit den Erzeugnissen der Fabrik besonders in England und Skandinavien Fuß zu fassen, aber die Fortführung des Unternehmens war nach achtjährigem Bestehen schließlich nur dadurch möglich, daß es in eine Aktiengesellschaft verwandelt wurde. Als solche nahm es im Jahre 1883 den seither in der weiten Welt bekannt gewordenen Namen „Hamburg-Amerikanische Uhrenfabrik" an. Die Direktion blieb in den Händen von Paul Landenberger, dem in den nächsten Jahren Herr Adolf Halbfaß aus Leipzig zur Seite stand. In einem Haupt- und einem Nebengebäude waren etwa 70 Maschinen für die Fabrikation von Uhren aufgestellt; das Aktienkapital betrug 160000 Mark.

❡ Nachdem so dem Unternehmen die notwendigen flüssigen Mittel zugeführt waren, zeigte es sich in kurzer Zeit, daß der im Jahre 1875 in den Boden

10

der deutschen Wirtschaft gepflanzte Sproß durchaus gesund und lebens-
kräftig war. Binnen Jahresfrist schon hatte sich die Arbeiterzahl von 70
auf 150 vermehrt, und mit Genugtuung meldet der erste Jahresbericht nach
der Verwandlung des Unternehmens in eine Aktiengesellschaft, daß die
Ende 1883 auf den Markt gebrachten Muster sich großer Beliebtheit er-
freuten und deren Erfolg zur Schaffung neuer Modelle anspornte. — Der
stetig wachsende Umsatz bedingte schon im nächsten Jahr eine wesentliche
Fabrikvergrößerung; es wurde ein benachbartes Grundstück erworben und
der Maschinenpark erweitert.

◄ Im März 1887 trat Herr Adolf Halbfaß aus dem Vorstand aus; an seiner
Stelle wurde Herr Christian Landenberger, der damals in London war,
als Prokurist für das hiesige Geschäft gewonnen und die Londoner Vertretung einem mit dem Fache vertrauten Hause übertragen.

◄ Im Geschäftsjahr 1887/1888 überstieg der Umsatz den des Vorjahres um
ein Drittel, und man mußte sich zur Neuaufstellung einer größeren Zahl von
Maschinen entschließen. Dabei hebt der Jahresbericht unter anderem her-
vor: „Was uns auch im verflossenen Jahr zugute kam, ist der Umstand, daß
unsere Waren nicht allein nach dem Preise, sondern auch nach der Qualität
geschätzt wurden und wir infolgedessen nicht nötig hatten, dem Preisdruck
bis zur letzten Stufe nachzugeben." — Bestrebungen, eine gemeinsame Preispolitik der Uhrenfabrikanten des Schwarzwaldes durch Zusammenschluß
zu erreichen, schlugen fehl.

◄ Der Geschäftsgang jener Zeit war befriedigend. Die Zahl der Arbeiter
hatte 300 überschritten, und neue Fabrikgebäude stiegen empor. Die Welt-

11

ausstellung in Melbourne und eine Industrieausstellung in Hamburg wurden damals — wenn auch in bescheidenem Ausmaß — beschickt und die Güte der Erzeugnisse mit silbernen Medaillen anerkannt. Die verhältnismäßig niederen Preise für Uhren Ende der achtziger Jahre verstand das Unternehmen dadurch auszugleichen, daß durch vermehrte Arbeitsteilung und erhöhten Maschinenbetrieb die Produktion verbilligt wurde. Dadurch ließ sich auch wieder der Umsatz steigern, der im Geschäftsjahr 1890/1891 den des Vorjahres um ein Fünftel übertraf.

❡ Neue Zollregelungen in den Absatzgebieten zu Anfang der neunziger Jahre bedingten einen vorübergehenden Rückschlag, von dem allerdings die Uhrenindustrie weniger als andere Wirtschaftszweige betroffen wurde. Hoch erfreulich aber war, daß endlich die lang erstrebte Verbindung Schrambergs mit der übrigen Welt durch die Eisenbahn zustande kam. Wir können uns heute kaum vorstellen, wie umständlich die Anfuhr der Rohstoffe und der Versand der Uhren vor 1892 vor sich ging, wo alles mit Pferd und Wagen von und nach Schiltach (9 km) und noch früher von und nach Hausach (26 km) gebracht werden mußte.

❡ Den Aufstieg der gesamten deutschen Wirtschaft in der folgenden Zeit machte auch die Hamburg-Amerikanische Uhrenfabrik mit. Ihr Liegenschaftsbesitz wurde erweitert; die Zahl der Fabrikgebäude und Maschinen vermehrte sich ständig, wodurch auch der Umsatz wieder erhöht werden konnte. Die Zahl der Arbeiter stieg auf über 750. Der Mangel an Arbeitskräften in Schramberg machte schließlich im Jahre 1898 die Herstellung einzelner Uhrensorten und Uhrteile im benachbarten Alpirsbach notwendig.

12

Filiale Alpirsbach **9 40 172**

❡ Im letzten Jahr des 19. Jahrhunderts wurden neue Betriebserweiterungen durchgeführt. Unter anderem wurde ein Sägewerk und eine Tischlereianlage neu errichtet; die Betriebskraft wurde um 100 P.S. erhöht und die Maschinen für Tischlerei und Uhrmacherei vermehrt. Ein zweiter Dampfkessel mit 120 qm Heizfläche wurde in Betrieb genommen und Uferschutzbauten am Göttelbach sowie Weganlagen auf den Holzlagerplätzen hergestellt. Die bisher pachtweise betriebene Fabrikanlage in Alpirsbach wurde unter der Bezeichnung: „Hamburg-Amerikanische Uhrenfabrik Filiale Alpirsbach" zur Zweigniederlassung ausgebaut und schließlich käuflich erworben (1900/1901). ❡ In dieser Zeit wurde das Schramberger Unternehmen durch einen Brand-

13

Plate 4
Factory branch in Alpirsbach

40

Wasserkraftwerk im Bernecktal

schaden heimgesucht, der jedoch für die ungestörte Fabrikation deshalb nicht so fühlbar wurde, weil damals ohnehin das gesamte Geschäftsleben, besonders in Deutschland, darniederlag.

❑ Bei Gründung der Aktiengesellschaft war als Geschäftssitz Hamburg gewählt worden. Mit dem Wachsen der Fabrik hatten sich dadurch manche geschäftliche Schwierigkeiten ergeben, denen man ein Ende machte, indem 1901 Schramberg zum Sitz der Gesellschaft erklärt wurde. — Die nächsten Jahre brachten einen wechselnden Geschäftsgang, der im ganzen aber eine Neigung zur Besserung zeigte. Es wurden neue Fabrikgebäude erstellt, und man suchte dem Arbeitermangel durch Wohnungsbeschaffung

14

Plate 5
Hydro-Power plant in
Bernecktal *(Also see page 101, plate 41)*

41

zu begegnen. 1903/04 wurde mit dem Ausbau der Wasserkraft im Bernecktal begonnen, und auch die österreichische Arbeitsstätte in Lauterach bei
Bregenz, die seit dem Jahre 1892 bestand, erfuhr eine Vergrößerung.
Auftragsausfälle, die durch den russisch-japanischen Krieg bedingt waren,
konnten durch Anstrengungen in anderen Ländern ausgeglichen werden. —
Ungünstige Zollmaßnahmen Frankreichs zwangen dort zur Einfuhr zerlegter
Uhren, wollte man den Boden nicht verlieren, den unsere Erzeugnisse gewonnen hatten. Es wurde deshalb in Paris eine Montierungswerkstätte
mit einer Verkaufsstelle gegründet. 1905 wurde das Kraftwerk im Bernecktal vollendet und brachte zur rechten Zeit eine Vergrößerung der Kraft-
quellen, denn die Produktion befand sich weiter in aufsteigender Linie. Der
fortschreitenden Erweiterung der Fabrikationsbetriebe entsprechend wurde
das Aktienkapital mehrmals erhöht. Auch in der Arbeiterzahl, die nun auf
über 1000 gestiegen war, drückte sich die Ausdehnung des Unternehmens
aus. Die gesteigerte Holzgehäusefabrikation bedingte eine Vergrößerung des
Holzlagers und die Erstellung eines Trockenhauses. Der Ausbau und die Verbesserung der übrigen Fabrikanlagen schritt folgerichtig fort, und 1910 wurde
die Aufstellung eines 325 pferdigen Dieselmotors notwendig.

❧ Im Geschäftsjahr 1911/12 wurde mit der Neueinrichtung der Tischlerei
begonnen, da die alte den durch die Mannigfaltigkeit der Uhrenmuster ge-
steigerten Bedürfnissen nicht mehr genügte. Die nächsten Jahre standen
unter dem Zeichen bedeutender Steigerung der Rohstoffpreise, der Löhne,
Steuern und sozialen Lasten, Ansprüche, denen gegenüber ein voller Ausgleich durch entsprechende Erhöhung der Verkaufspreise nicht möglich war.

15

Doch zweifelte niemand an der Überwindung dieser Schwierigkeiten und der weiteren gedeihlichen Entwicklung des Unternehmens, dessen Arbeiterzahl nun über 1300 betrug.

❡ Da kam der Krieg! — Binnen wenigen Wochen eilte mehr als die Hälfte der Belegschaft zu den Waffen. Es war für die Zurückgebliebenen keine kleine Aufgabe, den Gang der Fabrikation aufrecht zu erhalten, zumal die Abgeschlossenheit Deutschlands von den wichtigsten Rohstoffquellen den Staat zur Beschlagnahme von Messing und Kupfer für die Bedürfnisse der Kriegführung zwang. Sollte in der Heimat nicht Arbeitslosigkeit eintreten, mußte für die Uhrenfabrikation anderes Material verwendet werden. So wurde das Messing im Uhrwerk mehr und mehr vom Eisen abgelöst, womit allerdings die Qualität der Erzeugnisse nicht gesteigert, immerhin aber — trotz der Not der Zeit — ein Weg gefunden war, die Wünsche der Kundschaft zu befriedigen.

❡ Auch nachdem die erste, durch den Kriegsausbruch verursachte Stockung überwunden war, ging der Umsatz in Uhren natürlich wesentlich zurück. An seine Stelle traten immer mehr Lieferungen für das Heer, die schließlich die Einrichtung von Tag- und Nachtschichten nötig machten. Die Zahl der Arbeiter stieg wieder — in erster Linie durch Heranziehung weiblicher Arbeitskräfte — von 550 auf 800. — Was damals in einmütiger Opferfreudigkeit vom deutschen Volk draußen im Feld und in der Heimat geleistet wurde, bleibt unvergessen, und gerade die Erinnerung daran läßt in uns heute, trotz unüberwindlich scheinender Schwierigkeiten, die Hoffnung auf einen neuen wirtschaftlichen und kulturellen Aufstieg nicht sinken.

16

43

◀ Das Jahr 1918 brachte das Ende des Krieges. Damit kehrte die Hamburg-Amerikanische Uhrenfabrik wieder zur reinen Friedensarbeit zurück. 86 ihrer Mitarbeiter hatten die Treue zum Vaterland mit dem Tode besiegelt.

◀ Auch die Nachkriegszeit war an schwierigen Problemen überreich. Jetzt, in den Jahren des Währungszerfalls und der Stabilisierung, kam der im Jahre 1906 zur Wahrung gemeinsamer Interessen gegründete „Verband der Uhrenindustrie und der verwandten Industrien des Schwarzwaldes" bei der Regelung der sich allmählich überstürzenden Lohnverhandlungen mit der Arbeitnehmerschaft immer mehr zur Geltung. Des weiteren führte die außerordentliche Knappheit der Hauptrohstoffe und die Aufgabe der Wiedergewinnung des Weltmarktes zum Zusammenschluß aller deutschen Uhrenfabriken im „Wirtschaftsverband der deutschen Uhrenindustrie". Dieser suchte durch gemeinsame Rohstoffbeschaffung für alle ihm angeschlossenen Firmen die Aufrechterhaltung der Betriebe zu sichern und eine gesunde Preispolitik durchzuführen. Wenn die Lösung der zweiten Aufgabe, die in der Form von Preiskonventionen schon in den Jahren 1895—97 und 1906—08 versucht worden war, auch nicht restlos gelang, so leistete der Verband im allgemeinen doch Bedeutendes für die heimische Volkswirtschaft. Heute steht im Vordergrund seiner Tätigkeit die Herbeiführung günstiger Handelsverträge für die Uhrenindustrie.

◀ Die politischen Veränderungen in Deutschland brachten auch für die Hamburg-Amerikanische Uhrenfabrik manche unruhige Stunde, aber der gesunde Sinn aller an ihr Beteiligten verhinderte größere, nicht wieder gut zu machende Schäden.

17

❏ Bei der jetzt erfolgenden Wiederanknüpfung der durch den Krieg unter-
brochenen Verbindungen mit dem Ausland war der gute Ruf der Pfeilkreuz-
Fabrikate eine wesentliche Unterstützung.

❏ Die wirtschaftlichen Zustände der letzten Jahre hatten manche Einrichtung in der Fabrikation veralten lassen. Um Ersparnisse an Transport-
löhnen und sonstigen Unkosten zu erzielen, wurde jetzt eine gründliche
Durchorganisation des Betriebes vorgenommen und bauliche Erweiterungen
durchgeführt. Um der Wohnungsnot zu steuern, wurde eine besondere
Wohnsiedlung gebaut und die Zahl der Werkwohnungen auf insgesamt 89
gebracht. Zur Erinnerung an die Inflationszeit erhielt die Hauptstraße der
Siedlung den Namen: Billionenweg. — Ferner wurde mit kräftiger Unter-

18

Plate 6
Housing project -Glasbachtal-

45

stützung der Hamburg-Amerikanischen Uhrenfabrik die Gründung einer allgemeinen Baugenossenschaft in Schramberg betrieben, die heute über 26 Wohnungen verfügt.

❡ Dem dauernd guten Auftragsbestand in den Jahren 1920—22 und dem wieder normalen Beschäftigungsgrad stand als negative Erscheinung die fortschreitende Geldentwertung gegenüber. Diesem Umstand wurde durch Erhöhung des Aktienkapitals auf 10,5 Millionen Mark Rechnung getragen.

❡ Im August 1922 feierte der Gründer der Firma die goldene Hochzeit, was den Anlaß zu verschiedenen Stiftungen für Unterstützungszwecke gab. An diesem Fest nahmen die Belegschaft der Hamburg-Amerikanischen Uhrenfabrik und die ganze Stadt Schramberg herzlichen Anteil.

❡ In das Jahr 1923 fällt als bedeutsames Ereignis der Entwicklung der Stadt Schramberg der Erwerb des Gräflich von Bissingenschen Geländes zwischen Bahnhof und Stadtmitte. Stadtverwaltung und Industrie — unter hervorragender Beteiligung der Hamburg-Amerikanischen Uhrenfabrik — haben dadurch neue Entwicklungsmöglichkeiten geschaffen, die unserer Fabrik in Zukunft sogar einen Bahnanschluß bringen können.

❡ Immer mehr entwertete sich das deutsche Geld. Von einer Arbeit mit Gewinn konnte längst nicht mehr die Rede sein, denn eine immer verwickelter werdende und unübersichtliche Steuergesetzgebung, der infolge der Inflation stets größer werdende Mangel an Geldzeichen — zeitweise mußte eigenes Notpapiergeld gedruckt werden, nur um die Löhne rechtzeitig auszahlen zu können — und die rechnerische Mehrarbeit mit den immer gigantischer ansteigenden Riesenzahlen zerstörten jedes vernünftige Verhältnis

19

zwischen produktiver und unproduktiver Arbeit. Die Inflation machte jede kaufmännische Kalkulation unmöglich, bis endlich, Ende 1923, nicht zuletzt durch die Entschlossenheit der deutschen Industrie, wieder ein wertbeständiges Geld geschaffen wurde. Gerade in Württemberg waren es die Industrie- und Handelsgoldnoten, die zuerst dem scheinbar rettungslos der Zerstörung preisgegebenen Wirtschaftsleben eine feste Stütze boten. Der Sturz in den Abgrund war in letzter Minute vermieden worden, aber damit hatte auch die schwerste Krisis der deutschen Wirtschaft begonnen. Allenthalben im Deutschen Reiche mußte Kurzarbeit eingeführt werden, und auch diese genügte nicht, um eine beängstigend große Arbeitslosigkeit zu vermeiden. Der Schwarzwald und die Hamburg-Amerikanische Uhrenfabrik im besonderen überwanden diese Zeit verhältnismäßig gut, und seitdem bewegt sich die wirtschaftliche Entwicklung wieder in einigermaßen normalen Bahnen. — ᴄ Das 50. Geschäftsjahr der Hamburg-Amerikanischen Uhrenfabrik wurde wieder mit einer Goldmarkbilanz eröffnet. Diese Bilanz gab Rechenschaft über den wahren Stand des Unternehmens. Sie zerstörte den Wahn der Nachkriegsblüte und deckte die Schäden der Kriegs- und Nachkriegszeit rücksichtslos auf, aber sie bot und bietet auch die Grundlage für neue ernste und Erfolg versprechende Arbeit.

20

CHAPTER XIV

Die Hamburg-Amerikanische Uhrenfabrik im Jahre 1925

IM Jahre ihres Jubiläums steht die Fabrik in Achtung gebietender Größe vor uns. Ihr Name „Hamburg-Amerikanische Uhrenfabrik" betont neben dem Produktionsziel den wichtigsten Stammort des ehemaligen Betriebskapitals, Hamburg, und das System der Fabrikationsmethode, das amerikanische. Die Neuheit des letzteren bestand seinerzeit darin, daß die Nordamerikaner zuerst in größerem Umfange die Herstellung von Rädern und Werkplatten aus Messingguß durch das Ausstanzen aus gewalztem Messing ersetzten und die maschinelle Herstellung der Laternentriebe aus Metall, im Gegensatz zu solchen aus Holz und den massiven Stahlvolltrieben, ausbauten. Damit war der Weg gebahnt für die Massenherstellung von billigen Großuhrwerken mit auswechselbaren Bestandteilen von gleichmäßig guter Beschaffenheit.

⊄ Die Hamburg-Amerikanische Uhrenfabrik ist eine Aktiengesellschaft mit besonderer Note. Die Aktien lauten alle auf Namen und sind im wesentlichen in Händen der Familie Landenberger und eines großen Kreises von Freunden und Bekannten des Aufsichtsrats. Ein Besitzwechsel findet kaum statt, so daß man fast von einer Familienaktiengesellschaft im weiteren Sinne sprechen kann. Dieser Umstand hat in den letzten Jahrzehnten wesentlich zur inneren Stärkung des Unternehmens beigetragen. — Das Aktienkapital beträgt heute 3000000 Reichsmark in Stammaktien und 5000 Reichsmark in Vorzugsaktien.

21

Paul Landenberger, geb. 1848 — der Gründer
der H. A. U., Ehrenbürger der Stadt Schramberg, Mitglied des Aufsichtsrats, seit 1919
im Ruhestand lebend.

Frida Landenberger, geb. Junghans, geb. 1851

❧ Beide haben ein an Arbeit reiches Leben hinter sich. Sie sind der Mittelpunkt einer großen

Familie. Fünf Söhne und fünf Töchter sahen sie heranwachsen. Otto, der zweitjüngste Sohn,

fiel im Kriege 1915, die übrigen Söhne sind in der H. A. U. tätig. Auch zwei Töchter, Frau Frida

Luschka und Frau Martha Gunsser, sind durch ihre Männer mit dem Unternehmen aufs engste

verknüpft. — Eine Enkelschar von 25 Köpfen und 6 Urenkel sehen in Verehrung zu den Stamm-

eltern auf und versprechen, in ihrem Geiste vorwärts zu streben.

22

Plate 7
Paul Landenberger,born 1848-The Founder
of the H.A.U.
Frieda Landenberger,ne Junghans,born 1851

Der *Aufsichtsrat* wird gebildet von den Herren

WILHELM DEURER, Württ. Konsul in Hamburg

als Vorsitzendem seit Gründung der Aktiengesellschaft 1883

W. DINTER, Hamburg, seit 1885

PAUL LANDENBERGER d. Ae., Schramberg, seit 1919

AUGUST RUEFF, Bankier i. Fa. Paul Kapff, Stuttgart, seit 1919, † 1925

PHILIPP WIELAND, Ulm, Geh. Kommerzienrat, Dr. ing. h. c., M. d. R. seit 1923

Frühere Aufsichtsratsmitglieder waren die Herren

A. STEFFENS, Hamburg, 1885—1894

FRITZ HÖPER, Hamburg, 1885—1890

AD. BIELING, Hamburg, 1891—1893

CHRISTIAN GUNSSER, Tübingen, 1894—1915

G. AD. FISCHER, Hamburg, 1894—1923

Der *Vorstand* besteht aus den Herren

Generaldirektor PAUL LANDENBERGER d. J.

Direktor PAUL GUNSSER und

Direktor RICHARD LANDENBERGER

Die *technische Direktion* liegt in den Händen des Herrn

KURT LANDENBERGER

23

Plate reference page 51:

Plate 9, major expansion
of the HAU factory complex

Plate 9a, Bernecktal facilities

Plate 10, Alpiersbach HAU branch
factory.

Plate 10

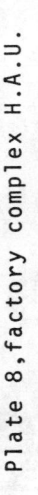

Plate 8, factory complex H.A.U.

Plate 9a

Plate 9

51

Plate 10a
Graphic by R.Nägele, year 1925
Sheet 20, of a 100 printing-Steel etching-
Private collection of the author.

Wilhelm Deurer,
Württ. Konsul, geb. 1850

❡ Er ist dem Gründer der H.A.U. in langer Freundschaft verbunden und seit Umwandlung der Firma Landenberger & Lang in eine Aktiengesellschaft Vorsitzender des Aufsichtsrats, in dem er stets in vorbildlicher Weise gewirkt hat und der sich auch heute noch seiner wertvollen Mitarbeit erfreut.

26

Plate 11
Wilhelm Deurer,Württ.Consul,born 1850

Paul Landenberger,
Generaldirektor, geb. 1875

☞ Er trat 1891 als Lehrling in die H.A.U. ein. Längere Aufenthalte und Reisen in der Schweiz, England und Nordamerika ergänzten seine kaufmännische Ausbildung. 1900 wurde er Prokurist, 1915 Mitglied des Vorstandes und 1921 Generaldirektor der H.A.U. Seine Persönlichkeit wurde im Lauf der Jahre immer mehr richtunggebend für den Geist des Unternehmens. Seit 1918 ist er Vorsitzender der Fachgruppe Großuhren des Wirtschaftsverbandes der Deutschen Uhrenindustrie.

27

Plate 12
Paul Landenberger,General Manager,born 1875

Paul Gunsser,
Direktor, geb. 1869

⊄ Er trat 1895 in die H.A.U. ein und wurde 1897 zum Prokuristen bestellt. Sein Arbeitsgebiet ist der Einkauf und damit verbunden die Überwachung der Rohstoffverarbeitung im Betrieb. Ferner gehört seine besondere Aufmerksamkeit auch heute noch der Versandabteilung, in der er einst seine Tätigkeit begann. Seit 1921 ist er Direktor.

28

Plate 13
Paul Gunsser,Director,born 1869

Richard Landenberger,
Direktor, geb. 1881

¶ Er trat 1899 als Lehrling in die H.A.U. ein. 1901/02 war er bei unserem damaligen Vertreter, Herrn O. Carry, in Paris, 1902/03 bei Landenberger & Co. in London tätig. 1904 kehrte er nach Paris zurück und kam schließlich 1906 endgültig nach Schramberg. 1911 erhielt er Prokura, seit 1921 ist er Direktor. Er leitet das Kalkulations- und Lohnwesen, ist Vorstand der Betriebskrankenkasse und betätigt sich in der Verkaufsabteilung. Er weiß kaufmännische Wünsche und technische Möglichkeiten einander anzupassen. Seit 1922 ist er Vorsitzender des Verbandes der Uhrenindustrie und der verwandten Industrien des Schwarzwaldes.

29

Plate 14
Richard Landenberger,Director,born 1881

Kurt Landenberger,
Diplom-Ingenieur und technischer Direktor, geb. 1878

⊄ Er unternahm 1904/05 im Auftrag der H.A.U. eine Studienreise nach Nordamerika und trat 1905 in die Firma ein. 1913 wurde ihm Prokura erteilt und seit 1921 ist er technischer Direktor.

30

Plate 15
Kurt Landenberger,Engineer Ph.D.& technical
Director,born 1878

Als *Prokuristen* der Firma sind tätig

Herr CHRISTIAN LANDENBERGER
Herr FRANZ GOEDE

Franz Goede,
Prokurist, geb. 1866

❡ Er trat 1896 in die H.A.U. ein. Nach fast 30 jähriger Tätigkeit ist sein Wirkungskreis die Aufsicht über die Gesamtbuchhaltung, die Bearbeitung der Steuerfragen und die Aufstellung der Bilanzen.

31

Plate 16
Franz Goede,Agent to sign in the principals
name or for the firm

AUF einer Fläche von 386 000 qm dehnt sich heute das Unternehmen aus. Dazu kommt noch die im Jahre 1899 gegründete Filiale für Weckerfabrikation in Alpirsbach. 2200 Arbeiter und Angestellte vereinigen sich, um die Pfeilkreuz- und Luxfabrikate in bester Ausführung herzustellen und in alle Welt zu senden. Ein Wasserkraftwerk mit 750 P.S. sowie zwei Dieselmotoren mit 775 P.S. und eine Dampflokomobile mit 120 P.S. versorgen das Werk mit der nötigen Kraft. Hunderte von automatischen Maschinen dienen der Erzeugung der mannigfaltigen Uhrbestandteile. Ein technisches Büro mit geschulten Konstrukteuren und Zeichnern sowie eine große mechanische Werkstätte widmen sich der Herstellung von Präzisionswerkzeugen und Spezialmaschinen. Die Metallgehäuse für Wecker usw. werden zum größten Teil in der eigenen Metallzieherei und -drückerei hergestellt. In hellen großen Räumen werden die Werke unter Nutzbarmachung jahrelanger Erfahrung zusammengesetzt. Ganz besonderer Wert wird auch auf die Regulierung der Uhren gelegt. Sie werden in verschiedenen Stadien der Fabrikation geprüft und dürfen die Fabrik nicht verlassen, ehe nicht ihr einwandfreier Gang bewiesen ist.

⊄ Die Tischlerei — fast eine Fabrik für sich — stellt Uhrgehäuse aller Art her, wobei der Auswahl des Holzes — es wird im eigenen Sägewerk geschnitten und in modernen Trockenanlagen getrocknet — besondere Aufmerksamkeit zugewendet wird.

⊄ Neben den gesetzlichen sozialen Einrichtungen bestehen Unterstützungskassen für Arbeiter und Angestellte sowie eine Badeanstalt mit einem Ver-

32

bandraum. Eine modern ausgestattete und gut geschulte Fabrikfeuerwehr ist stets bereit, die Arbeitsstätten bei Feuersgefahr zu schützen.

⊄ Insgesamt werden täglich etwa 5000 Uhren fertiggestellt (das sind, auf den Wecker umgerechnet, 15000 Stück täglich). Diese Zahl setzt sich aus allen möglichen Sorten von Großuhren zusammen, wie Wecker in Metall- und Holzgehäusen, Nippuhren, Kamin-, Wand- und Dielenuhren, Küchen- und Ladenuhren. Eine Spezialität bilden die von der Firma hergestellten Kurzzeitmesser für Telephonie, Chemie, Photographie und viele sonstige technische Zwecke.

⊄ In reger Zusammenarbeit mit ihren Abnehmern sucht die Leitung der Hamburg-Amerikanischen Uhrenfabrik die Bedürfnisse der einzelnen Länder zu erkennen und ihnen durch Anfertigung der gewünschten Muster Rechnung zu tragen. Entscheidend für das Anwachsen der Zahl ihrer Anhänger ist aber wohl die gediegene, technisch einwandfreie Arbeit ihrer Erzeugnisse.

⊄ Die weltbekannten Fabrikmarken der H.A.U. sind:

seit 1891 das Pfeilkreuz

seit 1905 die Öllampe (Lux)

33

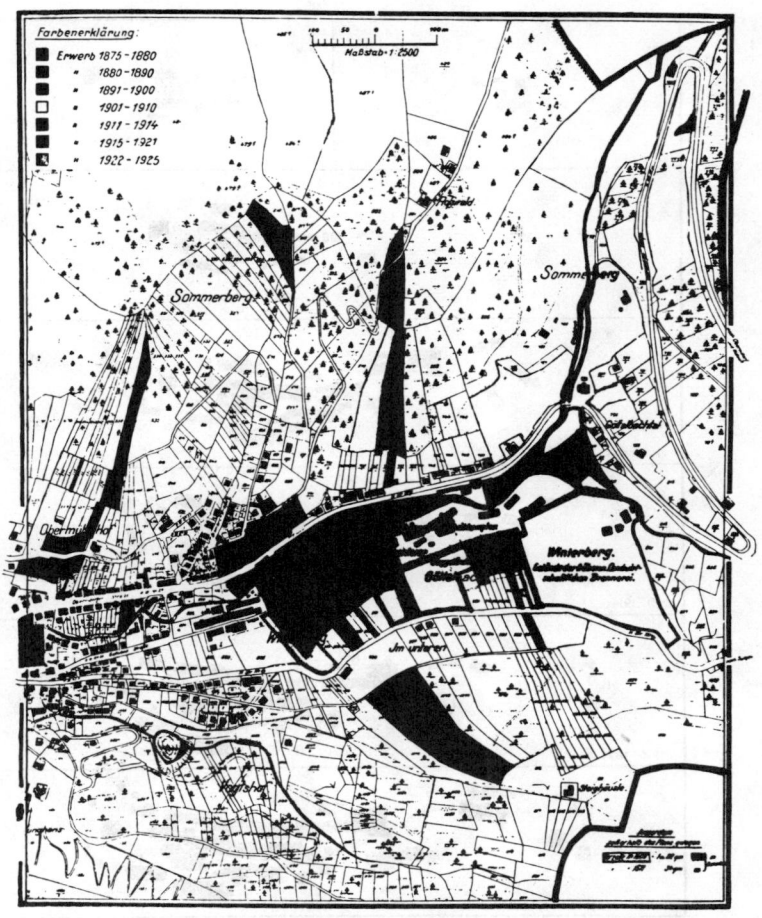

Grundbesitz der H.A.U.

34

Plate 17
Land and property of H.A.U.
    aquisition 1875-1880 aquisition 1911-1914
        "   1880-1890   "   1915-1921
        "   1891-1900   "   1922-1925
        "   1901-1910

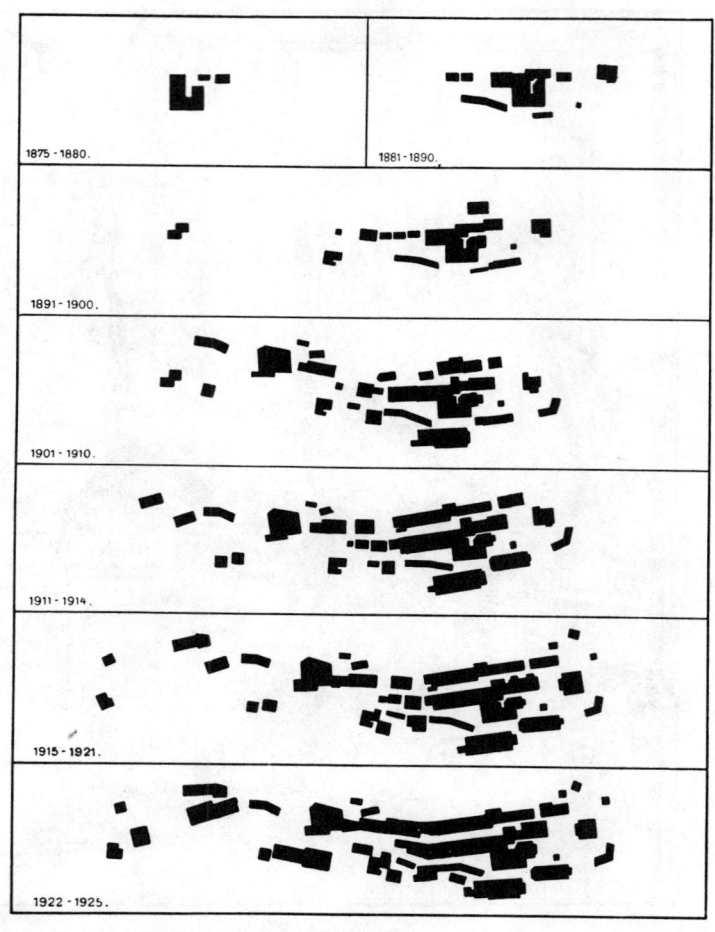

1875 - 1880.

1881 - 1890.

1891 - 1900.

1901 - 1910.

1911 - 1914.

1915 - 1921.

1922 - 1925.

Entwicklung der Fabrik, dargestellt durch die Vermehrung der Gebäude 1875–1925

35

Plate 18
Development and expansion of the plant
facilities buildings year 1875-1925

Vergrößerung von Kapital, Umsatz und Arbeiterzahl 1875—1925

56

Plate 19
Expansion of· capital,sales and persons
employed year 1875-1925

Treue und bewährte Mitarbeiter

INSGESAMT 174 Arbeiter und Angestellte blicken heute auf eine mehr als 25jährige Tätigkeit in der Hamburg-Amerikanischen Uhrenfabrik zurück. Aus vergangenen Jahren seien hier besonders genannt:

Viktor Luschka, #
geb. 1850, † 1914

❡ Er trat im August 1891 in die H.A.U. ein. In kurzer Zeit schon war überall in der Fabrik seine Eigenart, der Geist der Pünktlichkeit und Gewissenhaftigkeit zu spüren. Draußen bei der Kundschaft gewann sein liebenswürdiges Wesen manchen Freund für die Pfeilkreuzmarke, und besonders Österreich war ein Absatzgebiet, das er für unser Unternehmen neu erschloß. Im Jahr 1911 trat er gesundheitshalber in den Ruhestand. Vor seinem Tode im Januar 1914 durfte er noch erleben, daß sein Sohn Viktor Luschka in die H.A.U. eintrat. Seit drei Jahren ist dieser in Südamerika für die Pfeilkreuzmarke werbend tätig.

37

Plate 20
Faithful and outstanding members of
the Hamburg-American Clock Company.
(English translation see page 18&19)   # 12 64 173

Die Herren Daniel und Robert Friedel †

Sie machten sich in den Jahren 1895—1903 besonders um die Erweiterung der Geschäftsbeziehungen in Deutschland verdient.

Herr Wilhelm Hecht †

Er hat unserem Unternehmen durch seine Tätigkeit als Reisender in den Jahren 1905—1915 schätzenswerte Dienste geleistet. Vielen unserer Freunde wird er noch in guter Erinnerung sein.

Herr Paul Gunsser der Jüngere †

der älteste Sohn unseres Herrn Direktors Paul Gunsser. Er war im Auftrag unserer Firma erst in Hamburg und zuletzt in Hongkong tätig. — Dort hat ihn uns leider eine tödliche Krankheit vor Jahresfrist entrissen und damit schöne Hoffnungen zerstört.

Herr C. A. Hauser

Er war 1900—1910 Prokurist und technischer Leiter. Seine reiche Erfahrung auf dem ganzen Uhrengebiet hat viel zur Verbesserung unserer Erzeugnisse beigetragen.

Herr Jakob Hauser †

Oberwerkmeister 1879—1915. Er war lange Jahre Leiter des Maschinen- und Werkzeugbaus, auch lag ihm die Überwachung der technischen Fabrikeinrichtung ob.

Herr Fridolin Lehmann †

Meister im Werkzusammenbau in den Jahren 1877—1902.

Herr Erhard Günther †

Meister der Tischlerei in den Jahren 1880—1903.

Herr Karl Simon †

Meister der graphischen Abteilung in den Jahren 1886—1921.

Herr Alexander Hilser † 1893—1924

Er trat vor über 30 Jahren als Lehrling in die H. A. U. ein und stand zwei Jahrzehnte lang als Betriebsleiter der Uhrmachereiabteilung vor.

38

English translation see
chapter VII, page 18-19

65

Verkaufsorganisation

DER Absatz unserer Fabrikate vollzieht sich im In- und Auslande durch Vermittlung der Großhandlungen, wobei wir besondere Vertretungen in folgenden Ländern und Städten unterhalten:

Europa

Deutschland . . . . . . Berlin, Bremen und Hamburg
Bulgarien . . . . . . Sofia
Frankreich . . . . . . Paris
Großbritannien und Irland London
Jugoslavien . . . . . . Agram
Lettland . . . . Riga
Polen . . . . Warschau
Rumänien . . . . . . Bukarest
Spanien . . . . Madrid

Afrika

Südafrika . . . . . . Kapstadt und Johannesburg

Amerika

Vereinigte Staaten von Nordamerika: New York
Kanada . . . . Toronto
Argentinien . . . . . . Buenos-Aires
Brasilien . . . . Rio de Janeiro
Venezuela . . . . . . Caracas

Asien

China . . . . Canton, Hongkong, Shanghai
        und Tientsin
Japan . . . . Osaka
Britisch Indien . . . . Madras und Bombay
Niederländisch Indien . . Amsterdam und Rotterdam

Australien einschließlich Neuseeland
Sydney

39

English translation see
chapter VIII, page 19-20

66

❍ Hervorgehoben sei hier die Vertretung in Hamburg, die in Händen der Herren Deurer & Kaufmann liegt. Von den Teilhabern dieser Firma, den Herren W. Deurer, A. Lewerenz und A. Kaumann, ist Herr Konsul Wilhelm Deurer Vorsitzender unseres Aufsichtsrates. Die Verbindung mit „Deurer & Kaufmann" reicht bis in das Jahr 1878 zurück und hat unserem Unternehmen in dieser langen Zeit viele schätzenswerte Dienste geleistet. Seit dem Jahre 1919 vertritt uns in Verbindung mit „Deurer & Kaufmann" für China und Japan die China Export-Import- & Bank-Co., Hamburg.

❍ Hervorragend beteiligt an der Entwicklung unseres Unternehmens war auch die Vertretung in London. Von 1884 bis 1887 lag sie in den Händen des Herrn Christian Landenberger, der sie bei seiner Berufung nach Schramberg Herrn Th. Ascher übertrug. Er behielt aber auch fernerhin einen besonderen Einfluß auf das englische Geschäft und übernahm nach dem Tode des Herrn Ascher im Jahre 1895 die Vertretung wieder unter der Firma „Landenberger & Co.". Seiner Tatkraft und seinem im besten Sinne streng kaufmännischen Geist ist es zu danken, daß unsere Marke in Großbritannien und seinen Kolonien heute an führender Stelle steht. Seit 1914 hat die Firma Ernest A. Combs unsere Vertretung in London, deren Teilhaber Herr Ernest Combs schon 1887 begann, sich dem Verkauf unserer Uhren zu widmen, und deren anderen Teilhaber, Herrn Hans Frutiger, wir auch schon seit 1896 zu unseren Mitarbeitern zählen dürfen.

40

Christian Landenberger,
Prokurist, geb. 1859

❡ Er gehört unserem Unternehmen seit dem Jahre 1875 an und stand seinem Bruder Paul immer treu zur Seite. Im Auftrag der Firma war er 1879—1881 in Paris, 1883—1884 in Hamburg, 1884—1887 in London und von 1887—1895 wieder in Schramberg. Dann kehrte er nach London zurück und blieb dort, bis ihn die politischen Verhältnisse zwangen, England zu verlassen. Seit 1916 ist er wieder in Schramberg tätig.

41

Plate 21
Christian Landenberger,Agent to sign in
principals name or for the firm
(English transl.see page 20)

CHAPTER XVIII

Aus der Entwicklung der Großuhr in den letzten 50 Jahren

DIE Geschichte der Uhr reicht Jahrtausende zurück. Das Bedürfnis, die Zeit einzuteilen, sie zu messen, im Meere des ewigen Zeitablaufs einen bestimmbaren Standpunkt zu gewinnen, wurde mit den ersten kulturellen Regungen der Menschheit geboren, und es ist deshalb nicht verwunderlich, daß mit dem Eintritt von kulturellen Blüteperioden auch das Streben nach immer vollkommeneren Zeitmeßwerkzeugen wuchs. Wo früher eine Sand-, Wasser- oder Sonnenuhr Genüge leistete, wurde später die Räderuhr zur genauen Zeitansage benutzt. Und während in den Zeiten der langsamen Verkehrsmittel der Irrtum auch über längere Zeitabschnitte ohne Folgen blieb, bringt heute die Versäumnis von Minuten oder Sekunden oft schon die Gefährdung von vielen Menschenleben mit sich. Diese rasch steigende Bedeutung eines zuverlässigen, von allen äußeren Umständen möglichst unabhängigen Zeitmessers hatte zur Folge, daß die Technik früher als auf anderen Gebieten hier die theoretischen Probleme durcharbeitete und löste. Ja, man kann sagen, daß zu Beginn des vergangenen halben Jahrhunderts, das uns Anlaß zu unserem Rückblick gibt, der Organismus der Räderuhr seine endgültige Form gefunden hatte. Gewiß, die Zeitmeßkunst steht nicht am Ende ihrer Entwicklung — die elektrische Uhr, die drahtlose Übertragung von Schall und Kraft, wie sie die Radiotechnik gegenwärtig ausbildet, und manch andere Möglichkeiten zeigen neue Wege — aber die mechanischen Probleme der Räderuhr sind gelöst. Betrachten wir z. B. ein Weckeruhrwerk aus dem Jahre 1875 — wir beschränken uns hier entsprechend dem Produk-

42

tionskreis der Hamburg-Amerikanischen Uhrenfabrik auf Großuhren —
und vergleichen es mit einem solchen des Jahres 1925, so wird es dem fach-
lich nicht geschulten Auge schwer fallen, wesentliche Unterschiede festzu-
stellen. Die Fortschritte dieser Zeitspanne von 50 Jahren liegen eben mehr
auf dem Gebiete der Fabrikationstechnik als auf dem der Konstruktion:
❆ Aus den kleinen Anfängen industrieller Tätigkeit in den 70er Jahren
haben sich große Fabriken entwickelt. Wo einst wenige Dutzend Uhren
täglich produziert wurden, gehen heute Tausende in alle Welt. Und gerade
diese Produktionssteigerung schuf die Möglichkeit, Spezialmaschinen zu
bauen und zu verwenden, die bei leichter und geringfügiger Bedienung in
kürzester Zeit Arbeiten verrichten, die früher viele Personen nacheinander
in Anspruch nahmen. Diese Leistungsfähigkeit in der Produktion wirkte
hinwiederum fördernd auf den Absatz. Auch gab die fortschreitende Technik
des letzten halben Jahrhunderts nicht nur die Mittel zur quantitativen Entwicklung in die Hand, sondern sie hob auch weitgehend die Qualität der
Produkte. Dadurch gelang es im Laufe der Jahre, das Vorurteil so manches
Uhrmachers zu überwinden, der den „Amerikaner-Uhren" mit durchbroche-
ner Platine und mit dem Laternentrieb einst mißtrauisch gegenüberstand
und nur einem massiven Werk Zuverlässigkeit zuerkennen wollte — ein
Erfolg theoretischer und praktischer Kleinarbeit.

❆ Das Vorhandensein vollendet präziser Werkzeuge garantiert aber auch in
der Massenfabrikation die notwendige Exaktheit der einzelnen Bestandteile. Damit war die Voraussetzung gegeben, daß an die Stelle des früheren
primitiven Ausprobierens die technisch-wissenschaftliche Arbeit treten

43

konnte. Alle Rädereingriffe, alle mechanisch wichtigen Punkte des Werkes sind heute theoretisch gefunden und begründet; die Formen der Radzähne — bei den billigsten Uhren werden die Zahnräder fix und fertig aus dem Messingblech herausgestanzt — sind genau berechnet, wodurch die Zuverlässigkeit des Werkes bedeutend gesteigert wurde. Die technisch zweckmäßig konstruierten Uhrbestandteile verminderten die innere Reibung im Uhrwerk und ermöglichten eine erhebliche Kraftersparnis. Dadurch trat wiederum eine erwünschte Verringerung der Materialinanspruchnahme ein, die im Interesse der Billigkeit der Uhren eine Materialersparnis ermöglichte. Auf diesem Wege wurde das volkswirtschaftlich wichtige Ziel der zuverlässigen und wohlfeilen Uhr erreicht.

◅ Bei vielen, besonders bei den teureren Werken, wurden im Laufe der Zeit die Federn nach dem Vorbild der massiven Werke in Federhäusern untergebracht. Und bei Pendeluhren kamen neben dem ursprünglich alleinherrschenden Hakengang die auch verwöhnte Ansprüche befriedigenden Massivanker- und Grahamgänge auf. Die Zahl der Werksorten wurde — entsprechend den erweiterten Fabrikationsmöglichkeiten — immer größer. Zu den Schlußscheibenschlagwerken gesellten sich die Rechenschlagwerke. Durch die Verbesserung der Ton- oder Gongfedern lernte man mannigfaltige Klangvariationen erzeugen, und das Studium der Resonanz und der musikalischen Harmonielehre brachte, wie zum Beispiel bei dem modernen $^4/_4$ Westminsterschlag, eine neue Bereicherung und Fülle in die Schönheit des Stundenschlags.

◅ Die äußere Form der Uhr, das Gehäuse, ist als Teil der Wohnungsein-

44

71

richtung, in der wir leben, immer von den Geschmacks- und Stilwandlungen der Zeiten und Völker abhängig gewesen. Daraus erklärt sich die fast unübersehbare Fülle von Gehäusemustern, die ein Unternehmen wie die Hamburg-Amerikanische Uhrenfabrik seit ihrem Bestehen in die Welt hinausgesandt hat. Und auch die Zahl von etwa 800 verschiedenen Uhrensorten, die sie heute fabriziert, zeugt von dem Umfang der Anforderungen, die von überallher an sie gestellt werden.

◀ In dem Kampf um eine zeitgemäße Form all der Dinge, mit denen wir uns umgeben, ist Deutschland führend. Die Hamburg-Amerikanische Uhrenfabrik will auf ihrem Gebiet an der Veredelung dieser neuen Formen mitarbeiten, sie will, daß der Wert ihrer Erzeugnisse sowohl von einem technisch ausgezeichneten Uhrwerk als auch von einem dieses umgebenden geschmackvollen und formschönen Gehäuse begründet wird. Diese vollendete Einheit wird stets das Ziel ihrer Arbeit bleiben.

45

„Wo eine Spur nur von Kultur,

Findet man die Pfeilkreuz-Uhr"

Plate 22
Steel etching by R.Nägele,1925,with the
motto:

*"Where you find traces of culture
you find a Cross-Arrow clock"*

CHAPTER XIX
Historical data and documents.

Plate 24
Paul Landenberger
& Frieda Landenberger
ne Junghans @ 1870

Luschka Archive

NOTE:
Also see page 169 for
additional historical
data.

Plate 25
Paul Landenberger sen.
with authograph:
*"To my friend
   Alfred Luschka 1907"*

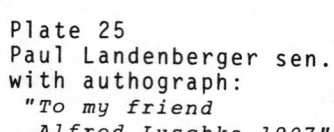

Luschka Archive

Plate 26
Paul Landenberger sen.
Schramberg
"To the oldtimer,the
Old vetran,many years
on the shipping dock
of the H.A.U.greetings
and good wishes for
the coming years!"
December 17.1885

Karl Weiss Archive

Plate 27
Paul Landenberger sen.
"Fortune up in the
next year"
(Birthday greetings)

13 75 171
13 75 173 *(German*

Plate 28
Paul Landenberger sen.
"Greetings to you for
the coming year"

75

Plate 29
Paul Landenberger,Frieda Landenberger(Center)
Standing:Left to right, Paul Landenberger jun.
                       Christian Landenberger,
                       Kurt Landenberger,
                       unknown,
                       unknown,
                       Richard Landenberger
Front row,seated:L.to r.Consul Deurer;
                       Paul Landenberger sen.
                       Frieda Landenberger,
                       Father of P.Landenberger
                       sen.

Plate 30
The Golden Wedding Anniversary 1922
l.to r.Paul Landenberger jun.Kurt Landenberger
       Paul Landenberger sen.Richard Landenberger
       & Fritz Landenberger

76

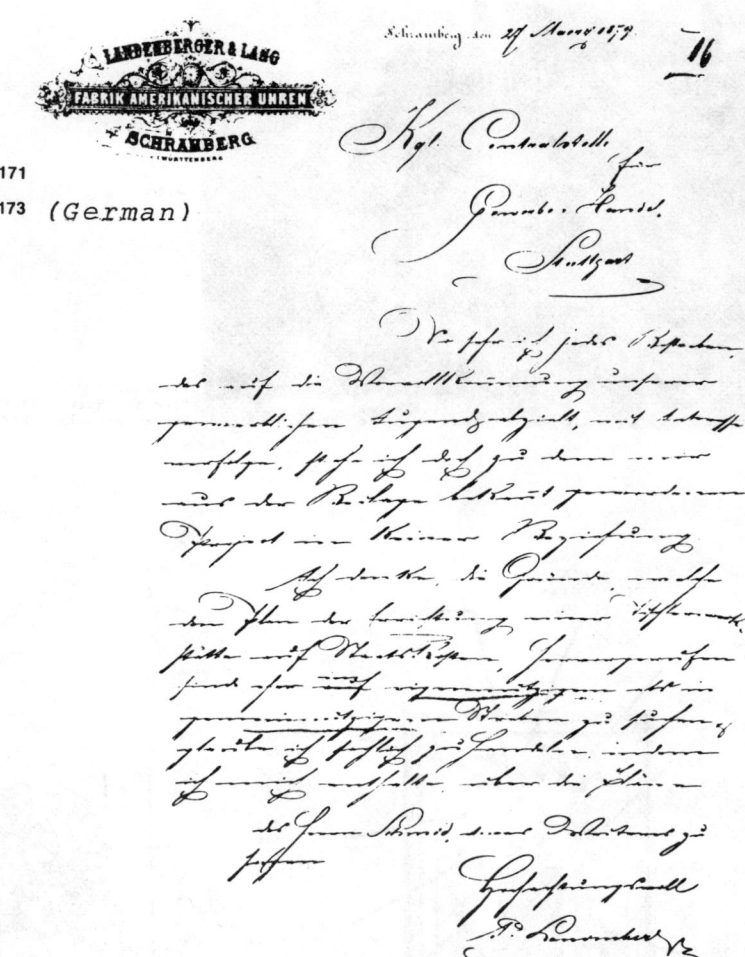

14 77 171

14 77 173 *(German)*

Contents of a handwritten letter by
Paul LANDENBERGER Sr.,dated 27.November 1879:

To the central OFFICE of COMMERCE in Stuttgart.
SCHMID,Superintendent of the Landenberger & Lang
Clock Factory has petioned the office in Stuttgart
to sponsor the installation of a TRADE SCHOOL for
cabinet makers and joiners in Furtwangen.
These efforts by SCHMID are received by
Paul Landenberger Sr.with mixed feelings.
Also see page 169 for additional archive evi-
dence.

Plate 31

Plate 32
"Inn and Hotel the Paradies"
Schramberg-Black Forest

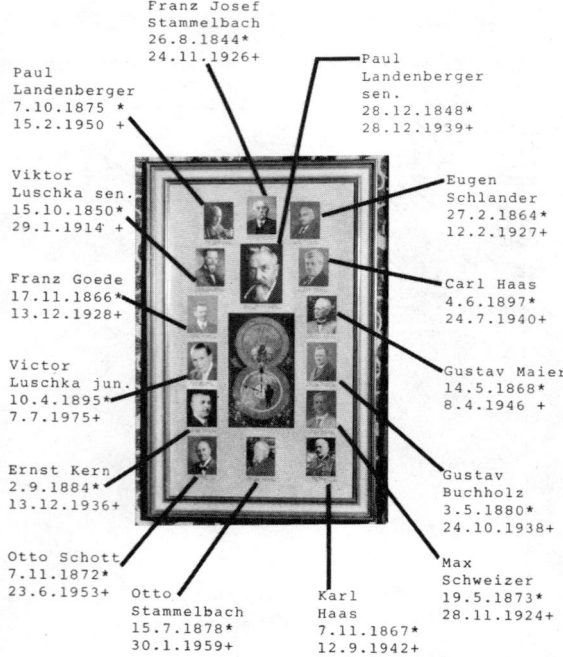

Franz Josef
Stammelbach
26.8.1844*
24.11.1926+

Paul
Landenberger
7.10.1875 *
15.2.1950 +

Paul
Landenberger
sen.
28.12.1848*
28.12.1939+

Viktor
Luschka sen.
15.10.1850*
29.1.1914 +

Eugen
Schlander
27.2.1864*
12.2.1927+

Franz Goede
17.11.1866*
13.12.1928+

Carl Haas
4.6.1897*
24.7.1940+

Victor
Luschka jun.
10.4.1895*
7.7.1975+

Gustav Maier
14.5.1868*
8.4.1946 +

Ernst Kern
2.9.1884*
13.12.1936+

Gustav
Buchholz
3.5.1880*
24.10.1938+

Otto Schott
7.11.1872*
23.6.1953+

Otto
Stammelbach
15.7.1878*
30.1.1959+

Karl
Haas
7.11.1867*
12.9.1942+

Max
Schweizer
19.5.1873*
28.11.1924+

Plate 34
Coat of arms of the:
STAMMELBACH family, owner since
many generations of the notable
inn & hotel "THE PARADIES"

Plate 33
The "Permanent corner table"
of the H.A.U.roundtable in the
"Paradies"

78

TABLE I   CHAPTER XIX

FOUNDING   AND   MERGER of the   HAMBURG AMERICAN CLOCK Co.

BROTHERS

** *CLOCK FACTORY*

GEBRÜDER
JUNGHANS GmbH
UHRENFABRIKEN
Schramberg
incorporated w.
DIEHL CORP.(1956)
Germany(W)

LANDENBERGER *
&
LANG
UHRENFABRIK
Schramberg
founded 1875

HAMBURG *
AMERIKANISCHE
UHRENFABRIK
(Since 1883)
1926 Cooperative
with JUNGHANS AG.
Schramberg,1930
merger with
JUNGHANS AG.

GEBRÜDER
JUNGHANS A.G.
UHRENFABRIK
Schramberg
Founded 1861

UNITED

***CLOCK FACTORY*

VEREINIGTE
FREIBURGER
UHRENFABRIKEN
(vorm.Gustav
  Becker)Freiburg
Founded 1847
merger w.JH 1926

STOCKHOLDER
CORPORATION
****CLOCK FACTORY*

AKTIENGESELL-
SCHAFT fur
UHRENFABRIKEN
Lenzkirch,founded
1851,merger with
Junghans 1927

NOTE:All titles* registered under the German name.
                    Reference ONLY
      ** For reference see:"JUNGHANS STORY"
      *** For reference see:"GUSTAV BECKER"STORY,and
          25 YEARS UNITED FREIBURG CLOCK FACTORIES"
      **** For reference see:"THE LENZKIRCH"and
                            "THE WINTERHALDER"Clock
                              enterprise.
      All published by ANTIQUE CLOCKs PUBLISHING
                CONCORD California.

TABLE II   CHAPTER XIX

HOLLAND

GERMAN
DEMOCRATIC
REPUBLIC

POLAND

Berlin

BELGIUM

FEDERAL
REPUBLIC
GERMANY

Bonn

FRANCE

WÜRTTEMBERG
(State of)

Schramberg
Black Forest

AUSTRIA

SWITZERLAND

ITALY

O R I E N T A T I O N

M A P

LOCATION MAP

Baden-Baden
Karlsruhe

Nord-
Schwarzwald

Straßburg

Stuttgart

Stuttgart

Freudenstadt

Horb

Straßburg
Offenburg

Wolfach

Schiltach

Alpirsbach

Oberndorf

Haslach

Hausach

1823

1856

HAU

Stuttgart
Tuttlingen

Hornberg

1856

SCHRAMBERG

Gottelbach

Triberg

1878

1836

Rottweil

Freiburg

St Georgen

Villingen

Schwenningen

Tuttlingen
Bodensee

Main road
Bundesstraße
Railroad
Bahnlinie
Country road
Landstraße

0   5   10   15 km

kilometer
Maßstab 1 : 500 000
Scale 1:500 000

B 33
Singen
Bodensee
Schweiz

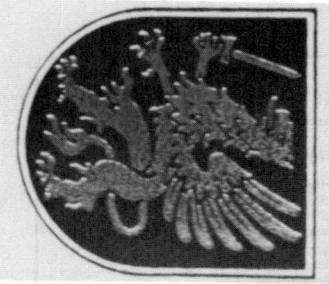

Plate 35
Schramberg, the
five valley city.
Founded @ 1547
City privilege
since 1867,
Population:
1731   1300
1846   3247
1871   4715
1890   7729
1910 10340
1925 14382
1933 14060
1939 16010
1950 16458
1961 18264
1966 18862

Luscka Archive

420 meter above
sea level
(1280 feet)

TABLE III   CHAPTER XX

TRADE SYMBOL or NAME	REFERENCE	REMARKS
	**Landenberger und Lang in Schramberg.** Königl. Oberamtsgericht zu Oberndorf a. N. Anmeldung v. 30. Oktober 1879, Vm. 9 Uhr, unter Nr. 2, für Uhrwerke, Uhrenbestandtheile aller Art, Zifferblätter, Uhrengehäuse. Bestandtheile solcher für Uhren aller Art, Uhren jeder Art, in fertigem und unfertigem Zustande: The KINGS Superior Court Oberndorf a.N.Registered October 30.1879,9 AM,under No.2	Refer to footnote: 15/82/171 15/82/173 (German)
	Initials on clock faces	
	HAMBURG =H* AMERIKANISCHE=A UHRENFABRIK =U SCHRAMBERG Registered: 10.2.1886	HAMBURG AMERICAN CLOCKFACTORY *abbreviated: H A U
HA U	since 1891	
	HAMBURG AMERIKANISCHE UHRENFABRIK in HAMBURG Reg.2.18.1892 in Hamburg	
	HAMBURG AMERIKANISCHE UHRENFABRIK in Hamburg Reg.2.29.1892 in Hamburg	

Plate 36A

TABLE IV

TRADE SYMBOL or NAME	REFERENCE	REMARKS
	HAU-HAMBURG Reg.7.28.1893	
	HAMBURG AMERICAN CLOCK COMPANY	= H = A = C *Label in clock:* *Württemberg independent State of Germany @ 1900
	HAMBURG AMERIKANISCHE UHRENFABRIK A.G. Schramberg since 1905	= HAMBURG = American = Clock factory = Stockholder Corporation
RELLAH (W)	HAU Reg.8.9.1906	
MAXIM (W)	HAU Reg.17.8.1907	
PHONOS (W)	HAU Reg.17.10.1907	
„Colonist"	HAU Reg.15.6.1909	NOTE: HAU abbreviated HAMBURG AMERICAN CLOCK Co.
„Sphären"	HAU Reg.12.8.1909	(W) = Word registration

Plate 36B

TABLE V

TRADE SYMBOL or NAME	REFERENCE	REMARKS
126107. ℔. 18123. „Hamburg-Amerikanische Uhrenfabrik In Schramberg"	HAU Re-register 2.4.1910	
INFANT (W)	HAU Reg.28.7.1910	
Phlox	HAU Reg.30.6.1911	
Pansy	HAU Reg.7.1.1911	
Chloris	HAU Reg.7.1.1911	
KOSMOS (W)	HAU Reg.1.10.1911	
Lux	HAU Reg.10.3.1911	
Diadem	HAU Reg.21.1.1911	

Timp	HAU
	Reg.30.6.1911
		NOTE: HAU
		      abbreviate
		
		HAMBURG
		AMERICAN
		CLOCK Co.
		
		(W) =
		      Word
		      registration

Plate 36C

TABLE VI

TRADE SYMBOL or NAME	REFERENCE	REMARKS
Placet	HAU Reg.30.6.1911	
Bucco	HAU Reg.7.11.1911	

TABLE VII - MOVEMENT PLATE INDENTIFICATION

FRONTPLATE

BACKPLATE

W 278

ABBREVIATIONS on CLOCKPLATES•ABREVIATION IDENFIFIER de ABKÜRZUNGEN an UHRENPLATINEN • HORLOGE PENDULE et MONTRE			
	GERMAN	ENGLISH	FRENCH
D.R.P.	DEUTSCHES REICHS PATENT	GERMAN PATENT	ALLEMAND BREVETS
D.R.G.M.	REICHS GEBRAUCHS MUSTERSCHUTZ DEUTSCHES	GERMAN TRADE SAMPLE	ALLEMAND NEGOCE ECHANTILLON
D.R.G.M. Angem.	DEUTSCHES REICHS GEBRAUCHS MUSTERSCHUTZ ANGEMELDET	GERMAN TRADE SAMPLE APPLIED	ALLEMAND NEGOCE ECHANTILLON SOLICITER
A.G. AKT.GES.	AKTIEN GESELLSCHAFT	STOCKHOLDER CORPORATION	CORPOEATION d ACTIONAIRES
G.m.b.H.	GESELLSCHAFT MIT BESCHRÄNKTER HAFTUNG	CORPORATION with LIMITED LIABILITY	CORPORATION a RESPONSABILITE LIMITEE
O.H.G.	OFFENE HANDELS GESELLSCHAFT	OPEN TRADE CORPORATION	SOCIETE de NEGOCE LIBRE
	VORMALS INCL.	FORMER INCLUDED	PRECEDENT INCLUS
GES. GESCH.	GESETZLICH GESCHÜTZT	PROTECTED BY LAW	PROTEGER par la LOI
ÖSTERREICHISCHES PATENTAMT WIEN		AUSTRIAN PATENT OFFICE VIENNA	OFFICE de BREVETS AUTRICHIEN VIENNE
D.G.M.S.	DEUTSCHER GEBRAUCHS MUSTER SCHUTZ	GERMAN SAMPLE PROTECTED	ALLEMAND NEGOCE ENCHATILLON PROTECTEUR
K.G.	KOMANDIT GESELLSCHAFT	REGISTERED CORPORATION Limited	REGISTRE CORPORATION ANONYME
E.G.	EINGETRAGENE GENOSSENSCHAFT	REGISTERED COOPERATIV	REGISTRE COOPERATIVE

ⓐ since 1891. Some movements have the model No embossed above TRADEMARK (TM)

or ⓑ since 1905 (LUX)

ⓒ movement model number

CHAPTER XVI

Technical Data.

The next pages offer functional diagrams of a few HAU
clock movements.These diagrams were developed and drawn
by Mr.G.F.Bley.

Who was Mr.BLEY? A clipping from the August 15,1930,
edition of the *"WATCH and CLOCKMAKER"*published in England,
provides an exellent biography of an watchmaker with outstanding expierence in many areas in addition to the technical practical field his handy drawings demostrate.
Mr.Bley was gifted with the graphic talent to introduce the problems with diverse clocks under the motto:
"ONE PICTURE IS BETTER THAN THOUSAND WORDS"
(l.c.after Confucius)

Harvey Silk Archive **16 86 171**

17 86 173

50 YEARS AS WATCHMAKER

CELEBRATING his 50th year as watchmaker, Mr. G. F. Bley, whose articles have appeared on occasions in WCM has found himself honoured in our German watch trade contemporaries by an account of his diverse experiences. Born in 1865, the son of a well-to-do watchmaker, he began at 15 to learn the business in Oldenbourg, Germany. His five-year apprenticeship ended he went to the watchmakers' schools at Glashutte.

After a year's service in the navy and a short stay in a chronometer business in Bremerhaven, he went south to Munich, and then still further south, to Milan, Rome, Naples, where he found other young watchmakers, enlarging their experience like himself. After two years in an unsuccessful venture in Hamburg to get taximeters for cabs introduced, he joined a Berlin firm who were putting up in public places electric clocks mounted on pillars. These suffered the same smashing and damage that his taximeters had received.

Things moved slowly therefore, and before long Bley was off to Nurnberg in an electrical works, designing water level indicators and telephones for special purposes. After three years Carl Marfels, the well-known and lately deceased watch collector, introduced him into the watch factory of Thiel Bros., in Ruhla, to work out new patterns based on an acquired patent.

Here he got to know the automatic machines used in the production of pocket watches. Next he assisted in the reorganisation of six small watch factories in Freiburg, in Silesia, into one concern. Automatic machinery for pinion manufacture was one of the steps introduced.

In 1902 he came to England to become technical director of a watch factory in Salisbury, bringing with him his family of three children. Here again, modernisation was undertaken, but unfortunately a fire eight years later burnt everything to the ground, and instead of being rebuilt the connection was moved to Coventry, where, however, he did not follow, returning instead to Germany. Here he has worked for twenty years in the Black Forest factory of the Hamburg-American Clock Company, learning the news on his 60th birthday, in 1925, of the loss of his many years' savings.

Plate 36E

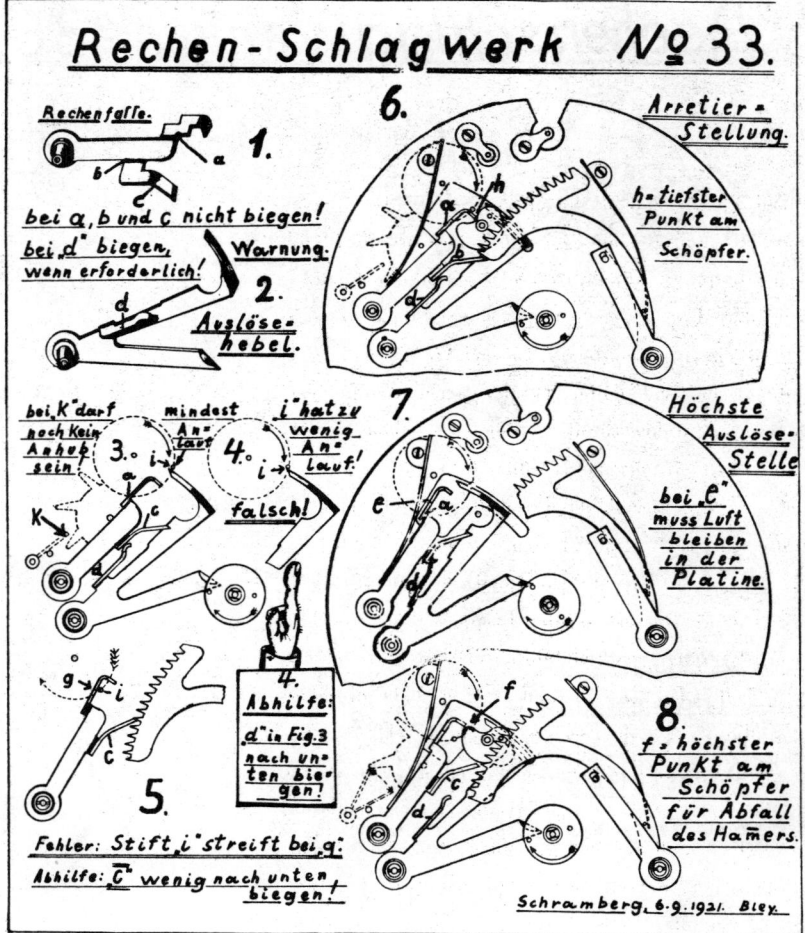

Rechen-Schlagwerk №33.

Plate 36

R A C̆ K   S T R I K E   M O V E M E N T No 33

1 Rack trap,do not make any attempts to BEND ⓐ,ⓑ, &ⓒ.
2 RELEASE LINK,bend ⓓ,only when required.
3 "K"position MUST be without LIFT motion,① minutes warning.
4 ① is in the wrong position,isufficient warning,correct bending ⓓ,Fig.3.
5 ERROR,pin ① is touching ⓖ.Correction:Bend ⓒ to the bottom(very,very gentle distance)
6 h= lowest point on the lifter.
7 HIGH point STRIKE release ⓔ must have min.clearance.
8 ⓕ high point on the lifter-READY for the first strike.

Rechenschlagwerk № 36.

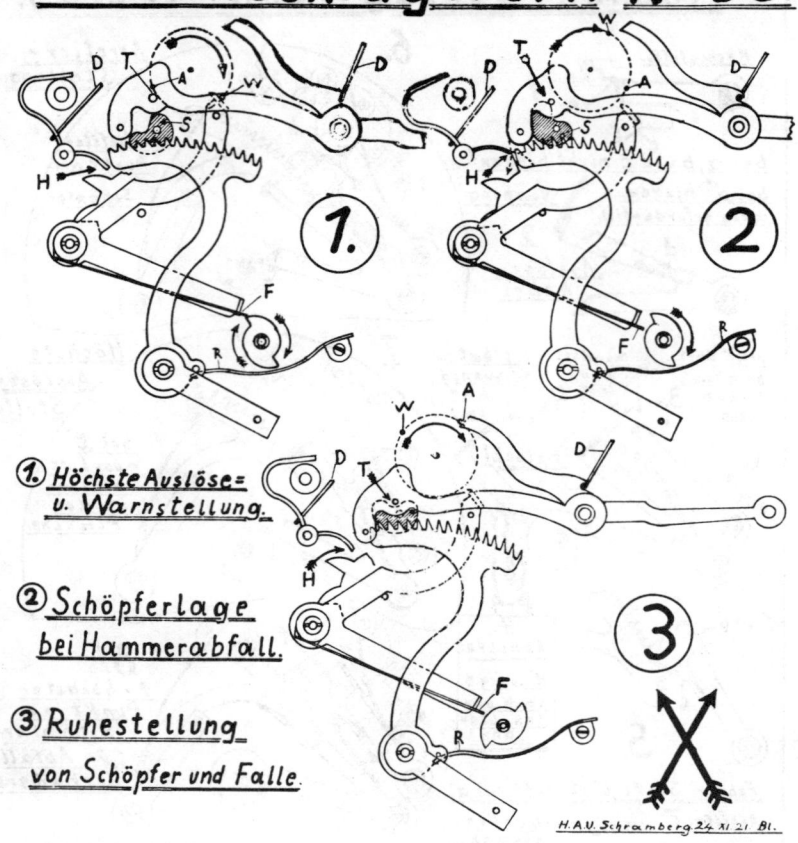

1. Höchste Auslöse= u. Warnstellung.

2. Schöpferlage bei Hammerabfall.

3. Ruhestellung von Schöpfer und Falle.

H.A.U. Schramberg 24 XI 21 Bl.

Plate 37

R A C K   S T R I K E   M O V E M E N T   No 36

1 High point release WARN-POSITION
2 Lifter position in a STRIKE FALL motion
3 NEUTRAL position lifter&lock lever.Note position
of the pin "T"and position of"A"warning wheel.

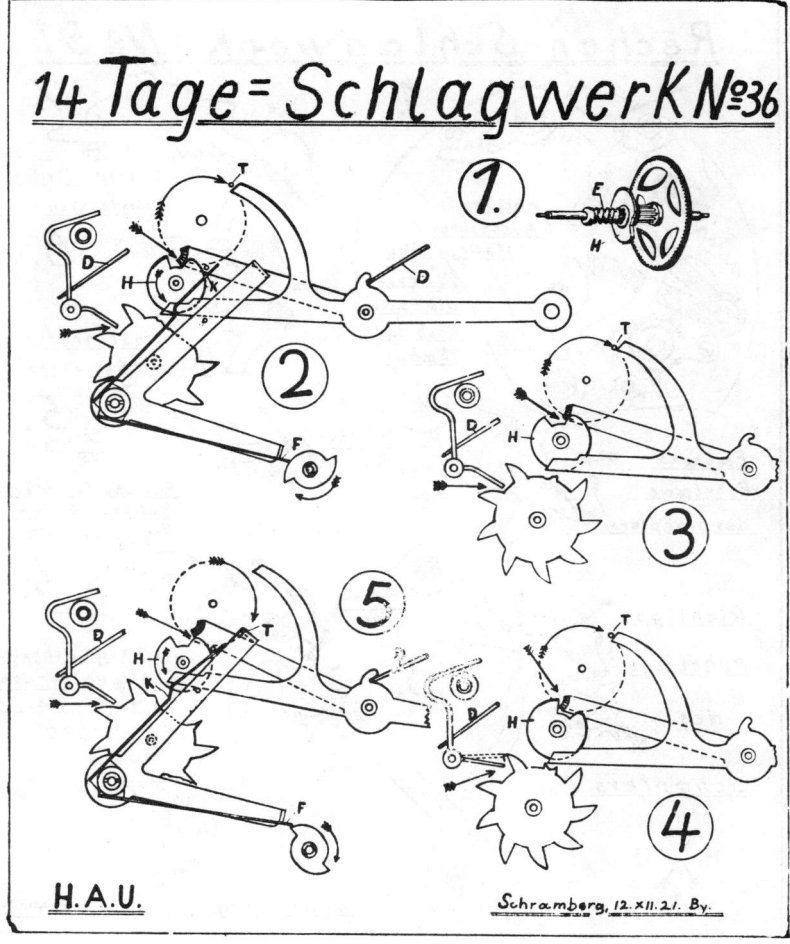

14 Tage = Schlagwerk K N̲º̲36

H.A.U.

Schramberg, 12.XII.21. By.

Plate 38

14 D A Y   S T R I K E   M O V E M E N T   No 36

1 Check tension of the strike RELEASE,spring "E" note
  disk"H" position.
2 High point release WARN POSITION,note position
  "T"- "K" - "H" & F.
3 Warning position note "T"&"H"
4 Very SHORTLY BEFORE strike release,note position"T"
  disk "H"& Starwheel release.

89

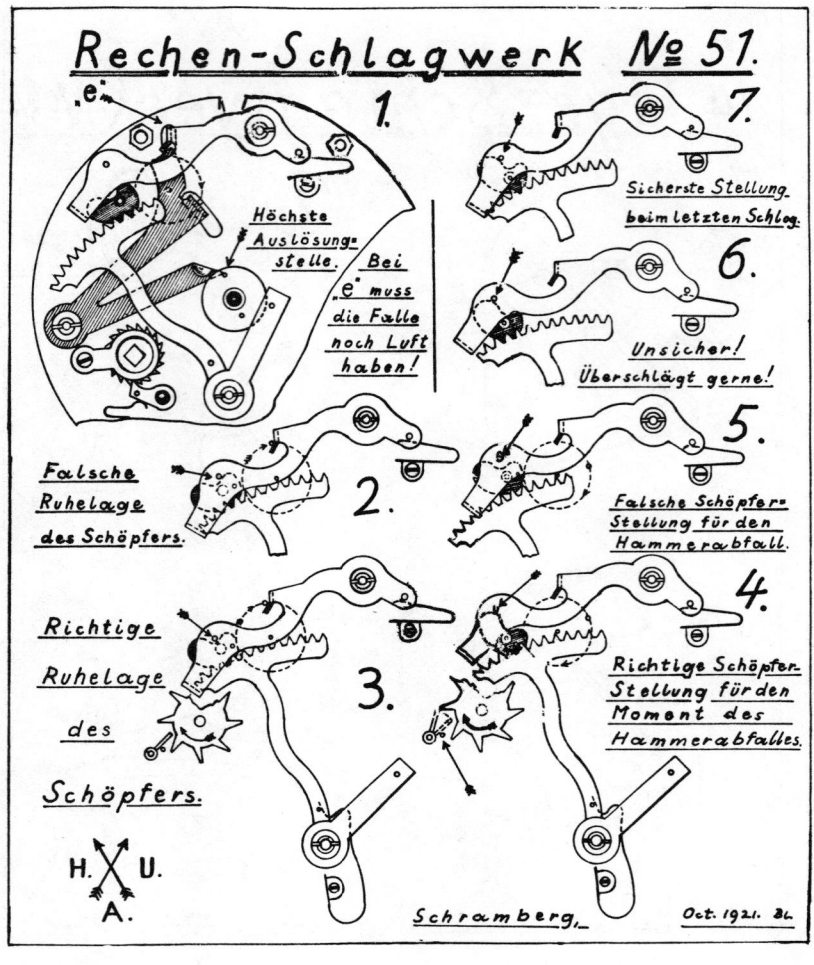

Plate 39
RACK STRIKE MOVEMENT No 51

1 High point strike release position ⓔ must have min clearance.
2 LIFTER in the WRONG pin position (Note the pointing of the arrow).
3 Perfect position of advancer.
4 Perfect position of advancer in the very moment the strike motion is activated.
5 WRONG position of the strike motion.
6 Weak adjustment of the the lifter pin.
7 Perfect position of the last strike motion.

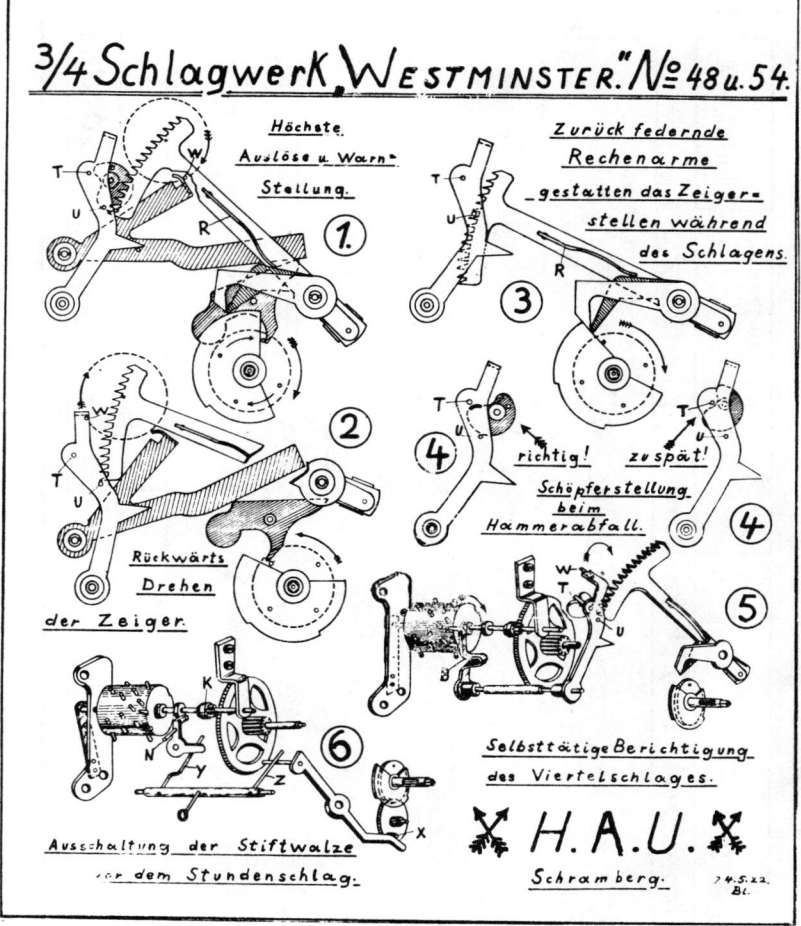

Plate 40

3/4 STRIKE MOTION "WESTMINSTER" No 48 & 54

1 High warning position
2 Release lever position,during backwards turning
  of hands.
3 The flatspring (R),attached on the leverarm of
  the rack allows hands adjustment DURING the strike
  motion.
4 Lifter position DURING strike motion,left,the right
  position shown,note the pin"T",4a late advance of"T".
5 Self adjusting correction of the 1/4 hr strike.
6 Position of the strike barrel BEFORE the hour strike.
  Note the position of"N"-"Y"-"Z"&"X".The pin wheel"K"
  is disengaged.

  GENERAL NOTE:It is very much recommanded to examine
              all positions of the strike 1/4 hr lever
              BEFORE any disassembling and or attempted
              CORRECTIONS.

91

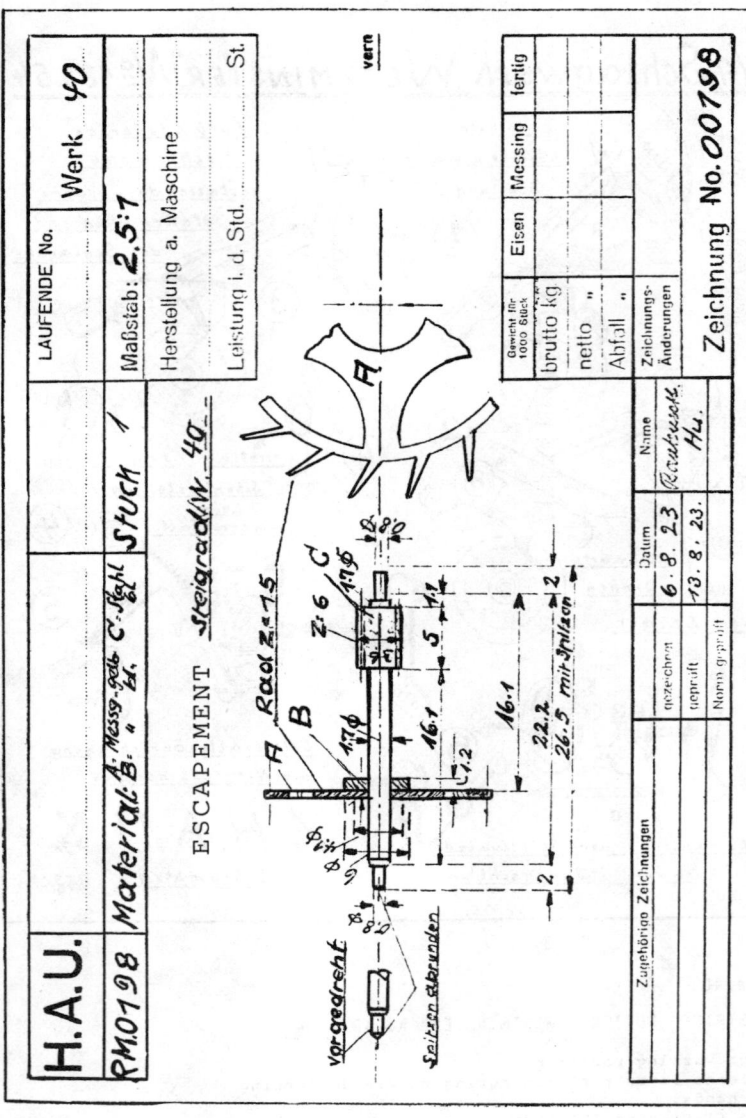

Plate 41
Typical HAU
shop
drawing

HAU-
Werkzeichnung

GRUPPEN 023, 024, 025
Wanduhren

Werk Nr. 277

Plate 42

Movement Nr.277,14 day half and full hr.rack strike
BIM-BAM.
14 Tage Halbstund-Rechenschlagwerk BIM-BAM.

Die Wecker auf Seite 12—20 sind ausgestattet mit unserem

PFEILKREUZ WERK No. 40

das durch besonders kräftigen Bau, mit Weckersatzrad, bequemerem Aufzug, mit feststellbaren Klappschlüsseln, den höheren Ansprüchen der Fachleute gerecht wird.

Auswechselbare Zugfedern.

The Alarms from page 12 to page 20 are equipped with our

CROSS ARROWS MOVEMENT No. 40

of solid structure, with intermediate wheel. Patent Snap Winders and easy winding, it is excellently suited to satisfy the requirements of the better class trade.

Removable springs.

Los despertadores de las páginas 12 a 20 llevan nuestra máquina

DOS FLECHAS CRUZADAS No. 40

que por su sólida construcción, con rueda intermedia en el mecanismo del despertador, facilidad para el remontaje del muelle, con llaves fijas de asas articuladas, reúne las mejores condiciones exigidas por los relojeros entendidos.

Muelles intercambiables.

Les reveils sur pages 12—20 sont munis de notre mouvement No. 40 qualité extra soignée avec notre marque de fabrique

DEUX FLÈCHES CROISÉES.

Ce mouvement se distingue par sa construction solide, une roue intermédiaire dans le rouage de réveil, par son remontage facile, par des clefs stables en remontant. Il suffit à toutes les exigeances de la clientèle la plus prétentieuse.

Ressorts démontables.

THE TRADE MARK CROSS ARROWS
LA MARCA DOS FLECHAS CRUZADAS
DIE MARKE PFEILKREUZ
LA MARQUE DEUX FLÈCHES CROISÉES

Removable spring, procedure without disassembling movement see page 103.

Plate 43
Cat.# D18
Year 1929

94

LUX WERK No.47
Ausgestattet das sich ver-
moege seiner sparsamen Bau-
art ohne Weckersatzrad fuer
diejenigen Kreise eignet,
die einen billigern Wecker
suchen.

LUX MOVEMENT No.47
Constructed on economical
principles without inter-
mediate wheel and with
smaller plates.They are
especially suited for cu-
stomers looking for a some-
what cheaper but neverless
reliable clock.

Wir verweisen bei dieser Gelegenheit auf unser Schmiermittel
»SAGITTOL« für Körnerschrauben,
das in allen unseren Ankerwerken
Verwendung findet und anerkannter-
maßen das Ablaufen der Körnerschrauben verhindert.
Auswechselbare Zugfedern.
(Siehe Seite 11.)

We specially direct attention to our
lubricant "SAGITTOL" for balance
screws which we have applied for more
than 15 years to all Lever-Movements.
It is a recognised fact that "Sagitol"
does not run away from the balance
screws and that it does not harden either.
Removable springs. (See page 11.)

Nous recommandons tout particulièrement notre graisse »SAGITTOL«
pour les vis de balancier qui s'emploie
depuis plus de 15 ans dans tous nos
mouvements à échappements circulaires
et qui empêche notoirement l'usure trop
rapide des axes de balancier.
Ressorts démontables. (Voir page 11.)

Les modèles sur pages 3—10 sont munis du mouvement économique No. 47 sans roue intermédiaire
avec notre marque de fabrique

LUX

ils sont tout particulièrement destinés pour la
clientèle recherchant à la fois le bon marché la
bonne qualité et le bon goût.

Los relojes representados en les páginas 3 a 10
llevan nuestra

MAQUINA LUX Nº 47

sin rueda intermedia en el mecanismo del despertador y con platinas pequeñas, que por su construcción económica es la indicada para quienes
desean despertadores de precio reducido.

Llamamos la atención sobre nuestra
grasa lubrificante »SAGITTOL«
especial para los tornillos de corr y
que se emplea en todas nuestras máquinas de escape áncora, esta d..
strado que no resbala por los c..os
Muelles intercambiables.
(Según página 11.)

THE TRADE MARK LUX
LA MARCA LUX

DIE MARKE LUX
LA MARQUE LUX

Plate 44
Cat.# D18
Year 1929

95

GRUPPE 019
Küchenuhren in Keramik
Kitchen and Nursery Clocks, earthenware plates and cases – Pendules pour cuisine en faience
Relojes para cocina en loza

KITCHEN and NURSERY CLOCKS

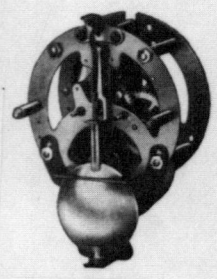

No.52
8 day pendulum movement
with transportation hold
in position pedulum
feature.
8 Tag Pendelgehwerk,mit
einfacher und sicherer
Transportbefestigung.

No.247
8 day pendulum time
movement,simple and
securely fastened
pendulum during trans-
portation.
8 Tag flaches Pendel-
gehwerk mit einfacher
und sicherer Trans-
portbefestigung.

Plate 45
Cat.Year 1930

96

Werke für Küchen-Uhren
Movements for Kitchen Clocks - Mouvements pour pendules de cuisine -

No. 19   No. 239   No. 68   No. 52

No.19
1 day lever time
movement,solid steel
pallets

Tag Anker-Gehwerk,
Massive Stahlanker.

No.239
8 day lever time
movement.

8 Tag Anker
Gehwerk.

No.68
8 day lever time
movement with
jewels.

8 Tag Ankergeh-
werk mit Stein-
koernern.

No.52
8 day pendulum time
movement.

8 Tag Pendel-Gehwerk

Werke für Studio-Uhren und kleine Wecker in Metall- und Holzgehäusen
Movements for Studio Clocks and small Alarm Clocks in metal and wooden cases
Mouvements pour réveils „Studio" et petits réveils en boîtes métal et bois
Máquinas para relojes de Estudio y despertadores pequeños en cajas de metal y madera

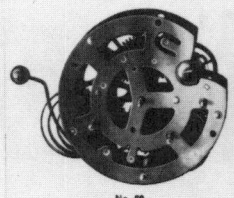 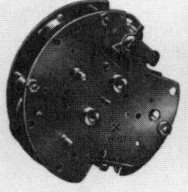  

No. 60
Platinen - Plates - Platines - Platinas
54 mm = 2⅛ inches

1 Tag Weckerwerk ohne Federhäuser
1 day alarm movement without barrels
Mouvement 30 heures à réveil sans barillets
Máquina 1 día de despertador
con cuerdas abiertas

No. 81
Platinen - Plates - Platines - Platinas
54 mm = 2⅛ inches

Flaches 1 Tag Weckerwerk mit massiven
Trieben, ohne Federhäuser
Flat 1 day alarm movement with solid
pinions, without barrels
Mouvement plat 30 heures à réveil avec
pignons massifs, sans barillets
Máquina plana 1 día de despertador con
piñones macizos y cuerdas abiertas

No. 79
Platinen - Plates - Platines - Platinas
54 mm = 2⅛ inches

Flaches 1 Tag Weckerwerk mit massiven
Trieben und auswechselbaren Federhausern
Flat 1 day alarm movement with solid pinions
and detachable spring barrels
Mouvement plat 30 heures à réveil avec
pignons massifs et barillets démontables
Máquina 1 día de despertador con piñones
macizos y tambores de cuerda desmontables

No. 44
Platinen - Plates - Platines - Platinas
50 = 42 mm = 2 × 1¹¹⁄₁₆ inches

8 Tag Anker-Gehwerk mit massiven Trieben
8 day lever time movement with solid pinions
Mouvement 8 jours simple à ancre
Máquina 8 días de cuerda à áncora

Plate 46
Cat.#31
Year 1930

97

Werke für Einsatz-, Marine-, Rund- und Büro-Uhren

Movements for Insert-, Ship-, Dial- and Office Clocks
Mouvements pour Pendules-Emboîtage, Habitacles de marine et Pendules de bureaux
Máquinas de Relojes para encajar, Relojes forma bitacora y Relojes de pared para oficinas

No. 68G

No. 74B

No. 74P

No. 77Q

68G
8 day lever-time move-
ment,platform escape -
ment with 7 jewels.

8 Tag Anker-Gehwerk
Echappement mit 7
Steinen.

No.74B
14 day pendulum
movement.

14 Tage
Pendel Gehwerk.

No.74P
Large 8 day lever
time movement.Plat-
form escapement w.
7 jewels.

Grosses 8 Tage
Anker-Gehwerk
Echappement mit 7
Steinen.

No.77Q
8 day lever rack strike
movement,platform esca-
pement with 7 jewels.

8 Tag Anker-Rechenschlg.
Werk Echappement mit 7
Steinen.

Werke für große Metall- und Holzwecker

Movements for large Alarm Clocks in metal and wooden cases
Mouvements pour grands réveils en boîtes métal et bois
Máquinas para despertadores en cajas de metal y madera

No. 250

No. 231

No.250
1 day alarm,small move-
ment.
1 Tag Wecker"Kleinwerk"

No.231
1 day alarm standard
movement.
1 Tag Wecker"Normalwerk"

Plate 47
Cat.#31,year 1930

98

OUR MOVEMENT for WALL= and MANTLE CLOCKS.

Unsere Werke für Wand= und Tischuhren

No. 61

No. 36

With countwheel or
rack. 14 day half-hr
8 and 14 day half-hr
strike.

Mit Schlusscheibe
oder Rechen.
8 und 14 Tag Halbstund-
Schlagwerk.

Full size plates,with
the feature of removable
spring barrels.
8 day 4/4 Westminster
strike.

Massive Platten und
Triebe.-Herausnehmbare
Federhaeuser.
8 Tag 4/4 Westminster-
Schlagwerk.

Plate 48
Cat.#30
Year 1934

99

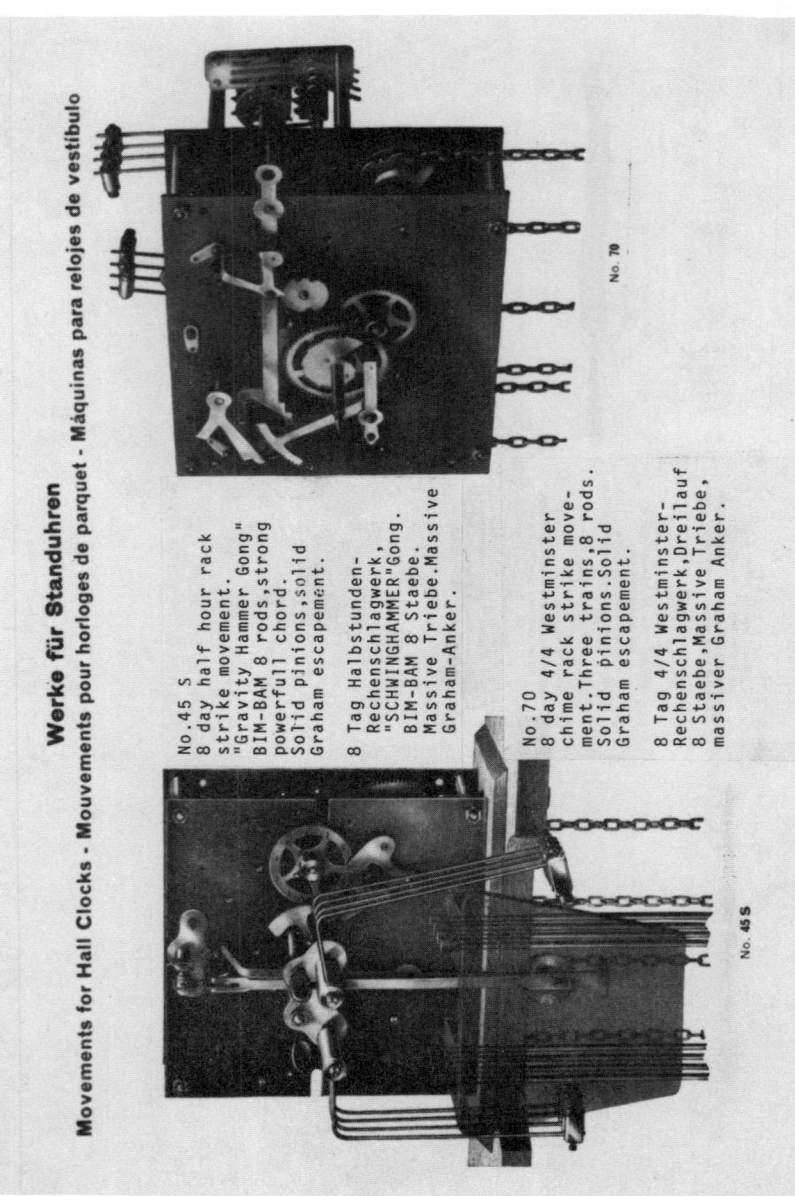

Werke für Standuhren

Movements for Hall Clocks - Mouvements pour horloges de parquet - Máquinas para relojes de vestibulo

No.45 S
8 day half hour rack
strike movement.
"Gravity Hammer Gong"
BIM-BAM 8 rods,strong
powerfull chord.
Solid pinions,solid
Graham escapement.

8 Tag Halbstunden-
Rechenschlagwerk,
"SCHWINGHAMMER"Gong.
BIM-BAM 8 Staebe.
Massive Triebe.Massive
Graham-Anker.

No.70
8 day 4/4 Westminster
chime rack strike move-
ment.Three trains.8 rods.
Solid pinions.Solid
Graham escapement.

8 Tag 4/4 Westminster-
Rechenschlagwerk,Dreilauf
8 Staebe.Massive Triebe,
massiver Graham Anker.

No. 70

No. 45 S

Plate 49
Cat.# 31
Year 1930

100

Werke für Wanduhren

Movements for Wall Clocks · Mouvements pour régulateurs · Máquinas para reguladores

No.64
4/4 Westminster chime movement with solid pinions.

4/4 Westminster Schlagwerk
mit Massiven Trieben.

No.77
Half hour rack strike
movement on ordinary
BIM-BAM gong.
Halbstund-Schlagwerk
auf einfachen oder
BIM-BAM Gong.

Auswechselbare Federhäuser — Exchangeable barrels — Barillets interchangeables — Tambores de cuerda desmontables

Plate 50
Cat.# 31
Year 1930

101

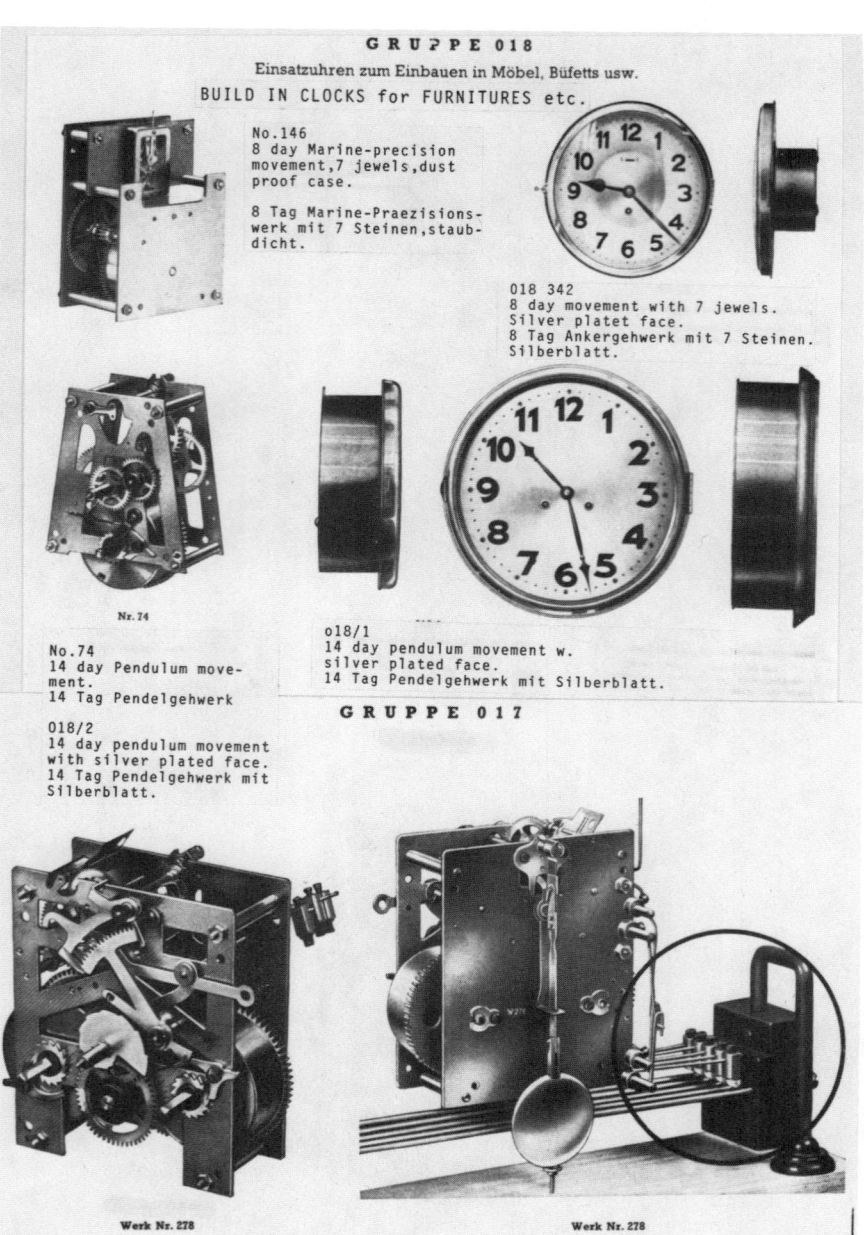

GRUPPE 018

Einsatzuhren zum Einbauen in Möbel, Büfetts usw.

BUILD IN CLOCKS for FURNITURES etc.

No.146
8 day Marine-precision
movement,7 jewels,dust
proof case.

8 Tag Marine-Praezisions-
werk mit 7 Steinen,staub-
dicht.

018 342
8 day movement with 7 jewels.
Silver platet face.
8 Tag Ankergehwerk mit 7 Steinen.
Silberblatt.

Nr. 74

No.74
14 day Pendulum move-
ment.
14 Tag Pendelgehwerk

018/2
14 day pendulum movement
with silver plated face.
14 Tag Pendelgehwerk mit
Silberblatt.

o18/1
14 day pendulum movement w.
silver plated face.
14 Tag Pendelgehwerk mit Silberblatt.

GRUPPE 017

Werk Nr. 278

Werk Nr. 278

Plate 51
Cat.#36

Auswechselbare Zugfedern

Seit Jahrzehnten sucht der Uhrmacher den Wecker, bei dem der Ersatz einer gebrochenen Feder leicht und ohne große Kosten vorgenommen werden kann.

Der Wecker ist da und die „auswechselbaren Zugfedern" der Pfeilkreuz- ✕ und Lux- Wecker sind in jahrelangem Gebrauch bewährt.

Es liegt nun nur am Uhrmacher, sich die Vorteile dieser praktischen Neuerung zu sichern.

Die Federn (Reparaturfedern genannt) sind in Drahtringe eingebunden (Abb. 1). Das innere gelochte Ende ist umgebogen, um leicht und sicher in den Haken der Federwelle eingehängt werden zu können. Das äußere Ende der Feder bildet eine längere offene Schlaufe.

Das Einsetzen der Feder ist **eine ganz einfache Arbeit.** Man läßt die Feder durch Entfernen des Drahtringes in ihre ursprüngliche langgestreckte Stahlbandform zurückspringen und hängt das gelochte Ende in den Haken der Federwelle ein (Abb. 2). Nun windet man die Feder durch Drehen des Aufzugschlüssels in ihrer ganzen Länge ein und schiebt die Schlaufe am äußeren Federende über den Platinenpfeiler (Abb. 3). Hiermit ist das Einsetzen einer neuen Feder schon beendet. Es bedarf weder des Abnehmens der Zeiger, noch des Zifferblattes, noch des Entfernens der Unruhe.

Die alte Feder entfernt man, indem man die vernietete Öse mittels eines durchgesteckten Hebels (Schraubenzieher oder dergleichen) aufbricht und die Feder herauszieht. Das abgebrochene, meist kurze innere Federstück faßt man mit einer Zange und zieht es nach Auslösung des Sperrkegels heraus. Die Pfeilkreuz- ✕ und Lux- Wecker werden jetzt alle mit den neuen Federn versehen, wo an die Stelle der Öse die offene Schlaufe tritt, die auch noch den Vorteil hat, daß sie sich bei ganz aufgezogener Feder gegen diese stützt, wodurch ein Ausreißen bei übermäßigem Aufziehen verhindert wird. Ferner wird das äußere Federende durch keine Lochung geschwächt.

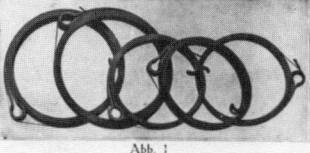

Abb. 2 Abb. 1 Abb. 3

Plate 52,Cat.O.3
Austrian Edition year 1927

REPLACABLE SPRINGS

NO disasemblement of the movement is required to ex-
change broken springs.The old spring can be removed
by prying the rivetend spring with an screwdriver,then
pulling the broken end with a plier(Good grip!!)while
holding the clickdog open.WEAR SAFETY GLASSES!
Note that the spring is held together with a wire ring.
The inner hole of the spring end is bentet to allow
SAFE and SECURE attachment to the spring arbor.The
outer part of the spring has an open loop.See Fig.(1)
    To insert the spring,remove the wire ring-CAUTION-
now the spring is an open end length spring.Attach the
hole end to the spring arbor.See Fig.(2).With the movement winding knob,wind up the entire lenght of the
spring,then attach the loop end over the movement
pillars,see Fig.(3).

Hausuhrgarnituren — Fittings for hall clocks — Garnitures pour horloges de parquet — Esferas, pesas y péndolas para relojes de vestíbulo

mit Nummern · and their numbers · et leurs numéros · con los números correspondientes

No 1
32 cm = 11 inches Ø
Silberblatt / Silvered dial / Cadran argenté / Esfera plateada ... No 1
Messingblatt / Brass dial / Cadr. cuivre jaune / Esfera de bronce ... No 32
Mattgoldblatt / Gilt dial / Cadran doré / Esfera dorada ... No 30

No 20
90 cm = 12 inches Ø
Silberblatt / Silvered dial / Cadran argenté / Esfera plateada ... No 20
Messingblatt / Brass dial / Cadr. cuivre jaune / Esfera de bronce ... No 40
Mattgoldblatt / Gilt dial / Cadran doré / Esfera dorada ... No 41

gedruckt / printed / imprimé / impreso = a
geätzt / engraved / gravé / grabado = b
oder / or / ou / ó = I

Pendellinse 150 mm
Pendul ball 150 "
Lentille 150 "
Péndola 150 " = I

No 2
32 cm = 11 inches Ø
Silberblatt mit gelber Mitte / Silvered dial brass centre / Cadran argentic centre doré / Esfera plateada centro de bronce ... No 2
30 cm = 12 inches Ø ... No 39

No 23 / No 22
32 cm = 11 inches Ø
Silberblatt aufgelegte Zahlen / Silvered dial raised figures / Cadran argenté chiffres appliqués / Esfera plateada cifras aplicadas ... No 23
Messingblatt aufgelegte Zahlen / Brass dial raised figures / Cadr. cuivre jaune chiffres appliqués / Esfera de bronce cifras aplicadas ... No 22
30 cm = 12 inches Ø ... No 45 ... No 34

No 6 / No 21
30 cm = 12 inches Ø
Silberblatt / Silvered dial / Cadran argenté / Esfera plateada ... No 6
32 cm = 11 inches Ø ... No 21

gedruckt / printed / imprimé / impreso = a
geätzt / engraved / gravé / grabado = b
= II

Pendellinse 120 mm
Pendul ball 120 "
Lentille 120 "
Péndola 120 " = II

Pendellinse und Gewichtshülsen, Messing geschliffen — Brass pendulum ball and weights — Lentille et poids cuivre jaune — Péndola y pesas de latín

Plate 53
Cat.# D18
Year 1929

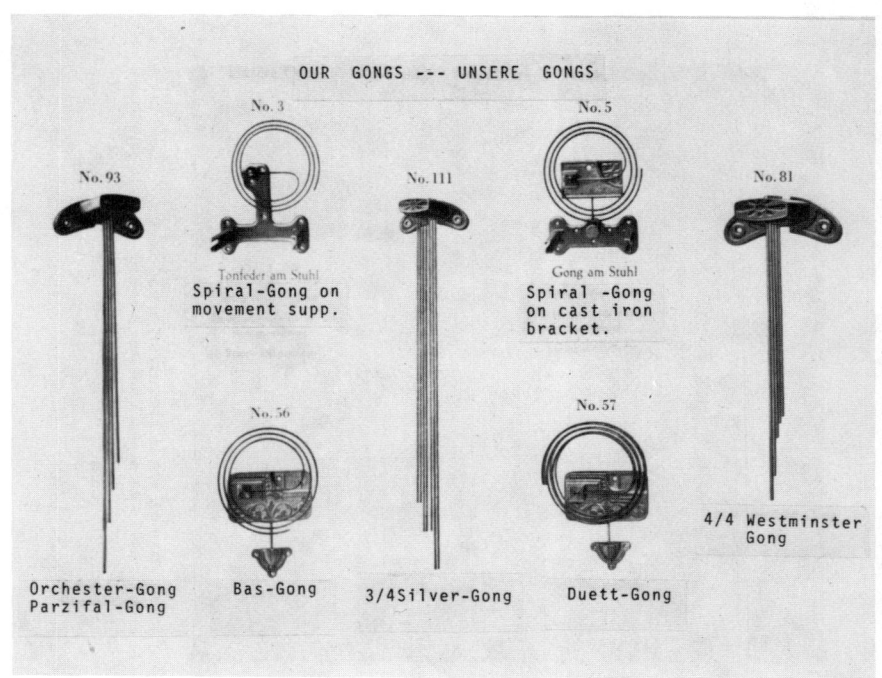

OUR GONGS --- UNSERE GONGS

No. 3 No. 5

No. 93 No. 111 No. 81

Tonfeder am Stuhl
Spiral-Gong on
movement supp.

Gong am Stuhl
Spiral -Gong
on cast iron
bracket.

No. 56 No. 57

4/4 Westminster
Gong

Orchester-Gong
Parzifal-Gong

Bas-Gong

3/4Silver-Gong

Duett-Gong

Plate 54,Cat.#D 18
Year 1929

DESCRIPTION of our GONGS

Bassgong,a beautiful gong,generally asked for.Orchestragong,
on four harmoniously tuned rod gongs.Parcivalgong"BIM-BAM"on
5 or 8 rod gongs.4/4 Westminster chime,striking the 1/4,1/2,
3/4,and 4/4 hour in one accord on 4 rod gongs.
(German)
Baßgong,schöner tiefer Gong mit einer Feder,die die allgem.
Ansprüche voll befriedigen wird.Orchestergong,wird auf 4 me-
lodisch abgestimmte Stäbe geschlagen.Parzivalgong,hat Doppel-
schlag"BIM-BAM"auf 5 oder 8 Tonstäben.4/4 Westminster Gong,
nach der bekannten Westminster-Melodie auf 4 Stabgongs,die
volle Stunde in einem Akkork auf 4 Stabgongs zusammen.

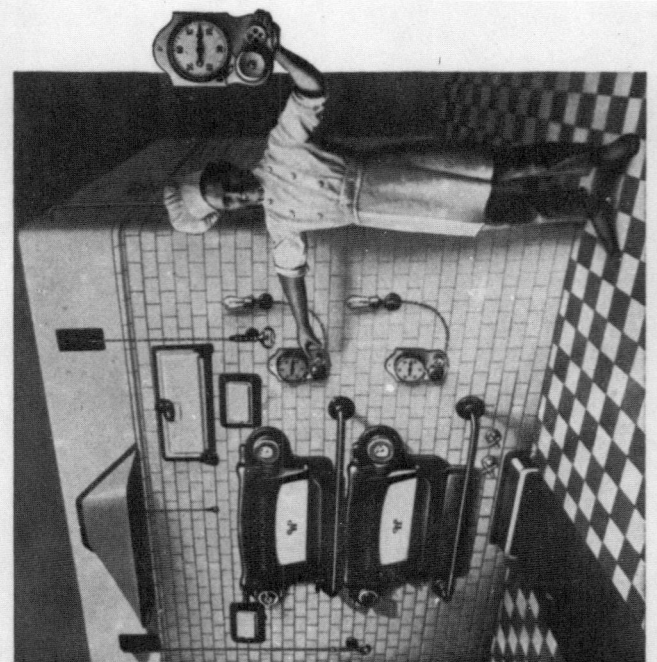

Nickelled brass case on white lacquered wood board - Dial under glass

Valuable for use in: Bathrooms, X-Rays examinations, for Dyers, Bakehouses, Breweries, Galvanic, Tempering and Vulcanizing purposes, all kind of Chemical, Physical and Technical observations, Colour Photography, also as Chessand Billiard Checker etc.

The admissible charge of this recorder is about 2½ Amp. maximum.
The recorder is supplied for continuous or alternating current with 110 and 220 Volt.

10″ × 6″, inches

No. 10714
Electric Time Recorder
Goes for 60 minutes

With bell signal and light signal
or for the starting of other electric apparatus
in the same or in another room
For checking spaces of time from 2 to 60 minutes
Automatic Winding by turning the hand
Stop and start lever

Plate 106
Cat.# K7
Year 1936-14
     1937

106

Plate 56a
Postman alarm clock

Plate 56b
"American type" movement

Plate 56c Black Forest
spiral gong

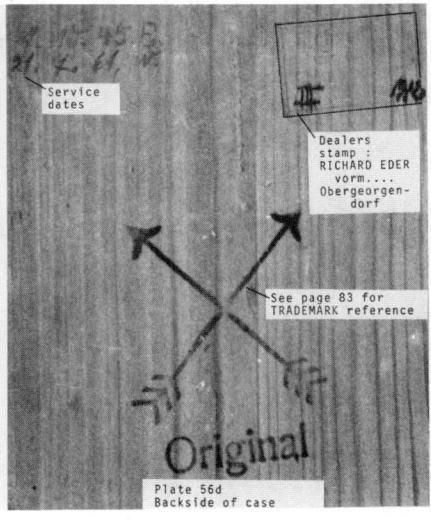

Service
dates

Dealers
stamp :
RICHARD EDER
vorm....
Obergeorgen-
dorf

See page 83 for
TRADEMARK reference

Original

Plate 56d
Backside of case

Plate 56a,56b,56c,56d
Year @ 1880

Private
Collection

189

Hamburg Amerikan Uhrenfabr.
Schramberg.

Schlußanspruch.

Schramberg d. ... 1898.

108 English translation
of the PATENT
APPLICATION
see page 109.

Plate 57

TRANSLATION of a PATENT APPLICATION

ADRESSE Landenberger

HAMBURG-AMERICAN CLOCK FACTORY

Schramberg(Black Forest)

.................189....

A cast-steelbody provides an anchor for clocks to which the anchorshaft,as well as the escapement wheel and the engaging pallets,are fixed attached.

HAMBURG-AMERICAN-Clock Factory

SCHRAMBERG

The submitted invention as described in figure 1 and 2 per attached drawing consists of an anchor (9a)for clocks from which is one piece of steel casting,wherein the shaft (b) as well as the escapement wheel and the pallets (c)and (d) are fixed in position with the anchor body during the casting process.

PATENT CLAIM:

One cast-steel body made from one piece wherin the pallets due to one-step casting process,are in a fixed position.

Schramberg,dated Nov.1898

HAMBURG-AMERICAN Clock Factory
Schramberg,November 24,1898

signed
Landenberger

Plate 57a

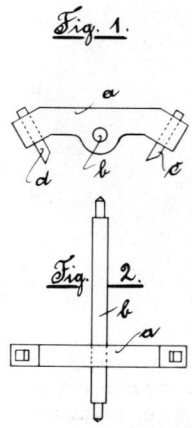

Fig. 1.

Fig. 2.

Hamburg- Amerikan. Uhrenfabrik

Schramberg d. 4 Novemb. 1898.

Hamburg-Amerikanische Uhrenfabrik.

110   PATENT APPLICATION
      see page 108 and 109.

Plate 58

CHAPTER XXIII-Production Facilities.

Dampfmaschinenanlage,200 PS
Aufgestellt 1889-1892

Plate 59
Steam engine,200 Hp,erected year 1889-1892

Turbinenanlage im Bernecktal,
440 PS,eingerichtet 1904.

Plate 60
Hydro-turbine,440 Hp,powerplant erected in
the year 1904

General Note:Plates 49 incl.62
Luschka Archive

Automatische Herstellung
der Triebe

Plate 61
Automatic machinery for gears

Zahnen der Räder

Plate 62
Gear cutting and rounding of gears

Plate 63
Square milling and riveting machines

Plate 64
Drilling and turning of parts

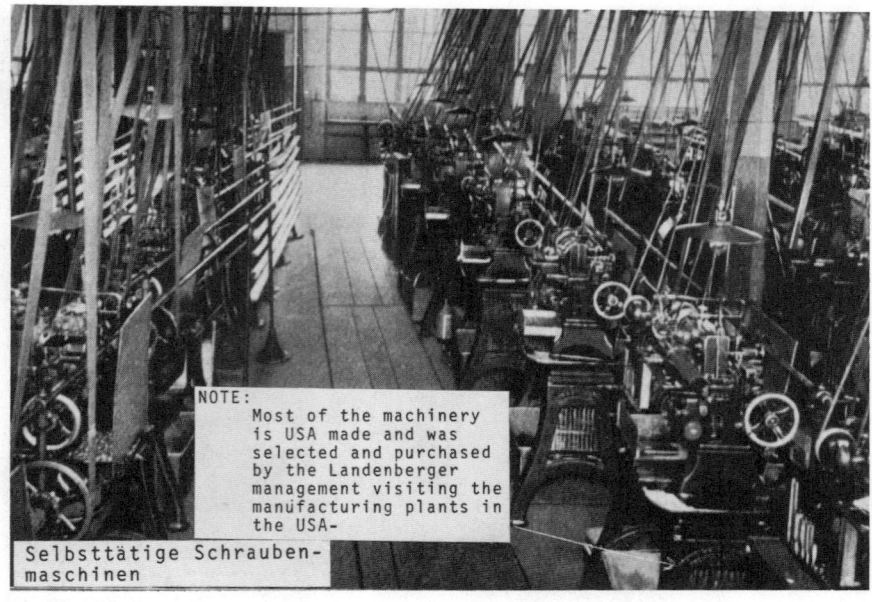

NOTE:
Most of the machinery
is USA made and was
selected and purchased
by the Landenberger
management visiting the
manufacturing plants in
the USA-

Selbsttätige Schrauben-
maschinen

Plate 65
Screw cutting automates

Automatische Fräserei
von Metallbestandteilen

Plate 66
Automatic milling of clockparts

Walzen und Prägen derselben

Plate 67
Rolling and stamping plant

Ausstanzen der Metall-
bestandteile

Plate 68
Stamping plant

Sägewerk,Durchschnittliche
Jahresleistung 3000 Festmeter
Tannenholz

Plate 69
Sawmill,98000 boardfeet anual milling
of Black forest pine

Zuschneiden der
Uhrenkasten Abt.II

Plate 70
Precut of clock cases

116

Rohberarbeitung der Hölzer

Plate 71
Milling of lumber

Zuschneiden der
Uhrenkasten Abt. I

Plate 72
Precut of details for clock cases

117

CHAPTER XXIV

Introduction to a selection of historical catalog
pages of the HAU- Company.

Penduluhr »Artista« 1877

Plate 72a
Early Landenberger &Lang
clock *-Private archive-*

The following pages have been selected from more than
one thousand catalog pages of the HAU Clock Company.
   With approximately three thousand model variations,
including clocks of all types,it is simply impossible
to reach a just conclusion as to what to show and what
should be classified of secondary interest.
   The dates on the catalog pages selected refer to
the printing date which is not neccesarely the year of
the clock model shown.
   To estimate the age of a clock shown on a catalog
page,it is safe to assume the clock is five to ten
years older than the catalog date.
   The clock models shown are selected from catalogs
with a printing date of 1927,1929,1930,1931,1933,1934,
1935,or 1936-1937.
   Earlier catalog data was not aviable since large
parts of the HAU factory complex were occopied by
military forces after 1945 and the stored archive
material in some parts simply disappeared.
   Further personal search of the author for catalog
archive material (Visit 1977)was declined by the owner
(Junghans-Diehl) of the former HAU factory complex.
   A few contacts with local poeple in Schramberg,the
author information obtained by others,that this
persons have "Old HAU"catalogs,were met with distrust
of the stranger from America.

   Due to the microfilming process,the lettering is
often slightly out of focus,or it is not perfect alig-
ned.This was beyond the authors control.

PENDULUM = CLOCKS
For office desk,parlor or ladies room

PENDEL=UHREN
FÜR SCHREIBTISCH, SALON ODER DAMENZIMMER

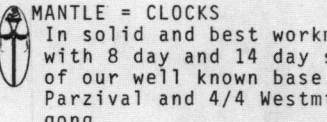

MANTLE = CLOCKS
In solid and best workmanship
with 8 day and 14 day strike
of our well known base,duett,
Parzival and 4/4 Westminster
gong.

KAMIN=UHREN
IN EINFACHER UND FEINSTER AUSFÜHRUNG
MIT 8 TAG UND 14 TAG SCHLAGWERKEN
MIT UNSEREM BEKANNTEN BASS., DUETT., PARZIVAL.
UND ⁴, WESTMINSTER-SCHLAG

No. 4008

80 × 33 cm = 11¾ × 13 inches

Marble =Imitation with brass decor,5" silver
platet dial,14 day movement,half and full
hour gong strike.

Plate 73
Cat.#D 18
Year 1929

119

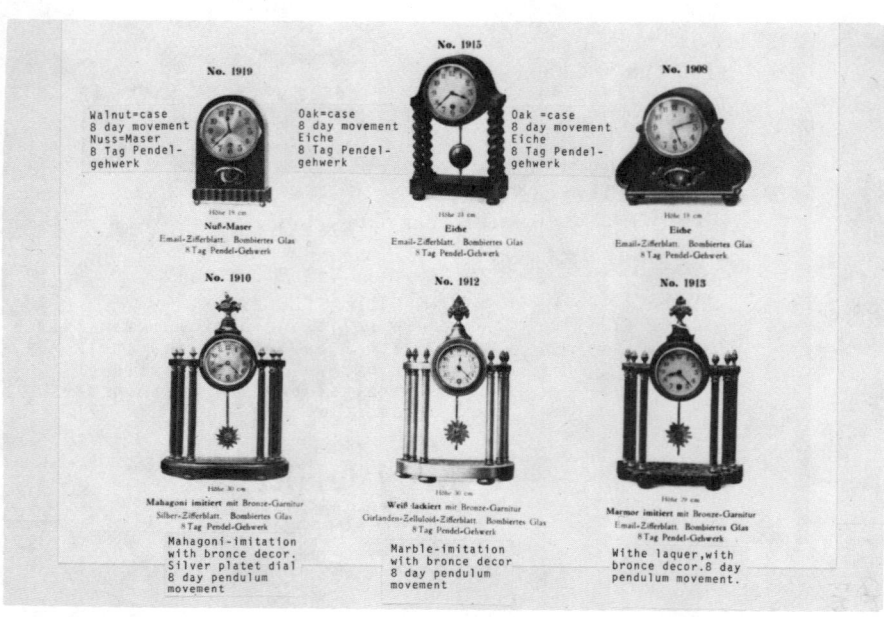

No. 1915

No. 1919
Walnut=case
8 day movement
Nuss=Maser
8 Tag Pendel-
gehwerk

Oak=case
8 day movement
Eiche
8 Tag Pendel-
gehwerk

No. 1908
Oak =case
8 day movement
Eiche
8 Tag Pendel-
gehwerk

Höhe 19 cm
Nuß-Maser
Email-Zifferblatt. Bombiertes Glas
8 Tag Pendel-Gehwerk

Höhe 18 cm
Eiche
Email-Zifferblatt. Bombiertes Glas
8 Tag Pendel-Gehwerk

Höhe 19 cm
Eiche
Email-Zifferblatt. Bombiertes Glas
8 Tag Pendel-Gehwerk

No. 1910

No. 1912

No. 1913

Höhe 30 cm
Mahagoni imitiert *mit* **Bronce-Garnitur**
Silber-Zifferblatt. Bombiertes Glas
8 Tag Pendel-Gehwerk

Mahagoni-imitation
with bronce decor.
Silver platet dial
8 day pendulum
movement

Höhe 30 cm
Weiß lackiert mit Bronce-Garnitur
Girlanden-Zelluloid-Zifferblatt. Bombiertes Glas
8 Tag Pendel-Gehwerk

Marble-imitation
with bronce decor
8 day pendulum
movement

Höhe 29 cm
Marmor imitiert mit Bronce-Garnitur
Email-Zifferblatt. Bombiertes Glas
8 Tag Pendel-Gehwerk

Withe laquer,with
bronce decor.8 day
pendulum movement.

Plate 74
Cat.# D 18,year 1929

Wecker in Metall-
und Holzgehäusen

Alarm Clocks in metal and wooden cases
Réveils en boîtes métal et bois
Despertadores en cajas de metal y madera

Plate 75
Cat.# 31
Year 1930

120

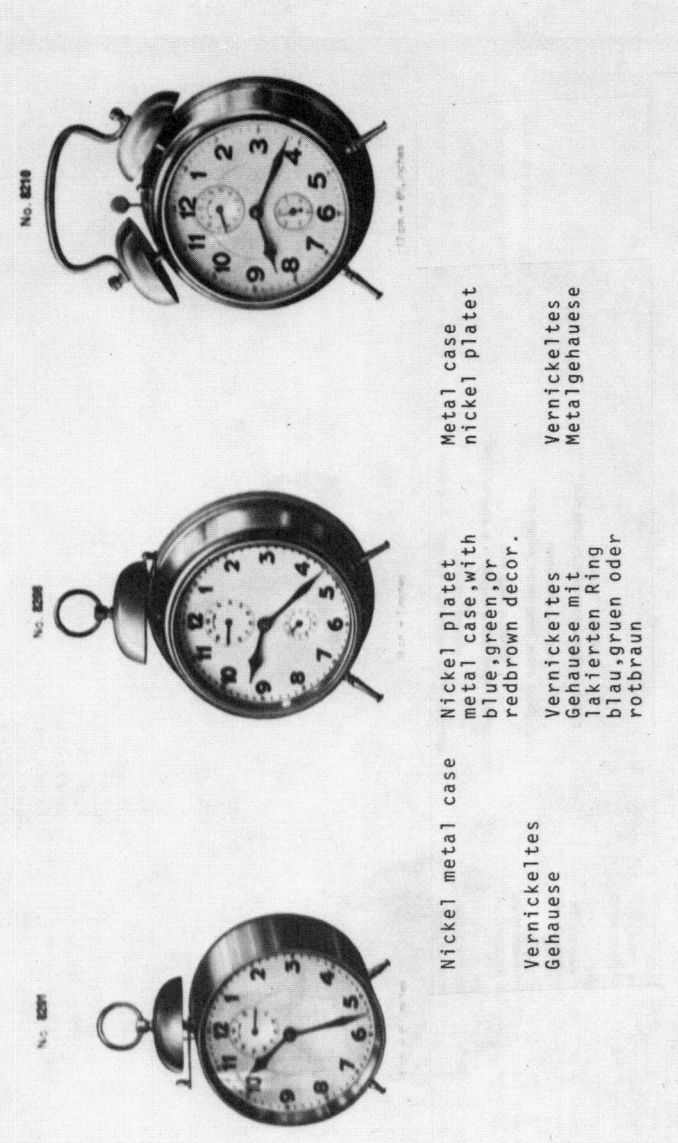

No. 8297

No. 8298

No. 8299

Nickel metal case

Vernickeltes
Gehauese

Nickel platet
metal case with
blue,green,or
redbrown decor.

Vernickeltes
Gehauese mit
lakierten Ring
blau,gruen oder
rotbraun

Metal case
nickel platet

Vernickeltes
Metalgehauese

Plate 76
Cat.#31
Year 1930

121

COLONIST

No. 9001 ½

12 Stunden-Blatt

12 hour dial

Höhe 18 cm

Zinkgehäuse vernickelt
vermessingte Rückwand

Weißes Zifferblatt mit oder ohne Radium

1 Tag Ankerwecker

No. 9001 ½

24 Stunden-Blatt

24 hour dial

hight 18 cm
Zinccase nickel
plated,white face
and dial,one day
movement
Zinckgehause
vernickelt,weisses
Zifferblatt,1 Tag
Ankerwerk

24 hour dial
24 Stunden=
Zifferblatt

No. 9001 ½

Flourocent=dial
Radium=
Zifferblatt

Plate 77
Cat.#D18
Year 1929

122

Markenlose Wecker

ALARM CLOCKS without TRADEMARK

Nr 9050

Nr 9045

Nr 9048

Nr 9059

Metal case,redbrown or
blue laquer,bell nickel
plated

Case nickel plated or
blue,green or redbrown
laquer

Metal case witout
seam,blue or red-
brown laquer

Metal case witout
seam,blue or red-
brown laquer

1 day alarm clock-white dial
without or with flourecent dial

1 Tag Wecker Weißes Zifferblatt, mit oder ohne Radium

Plate 78
Cat.#30
Year 1934

Wecker mit Rückwandglocke – Alarm clocks with bell at back – Réveils avec timbre au fond – Despertadores con campana atrás

LUXOR No. 184 Rep.

16 cm — 6¹/₄ inches.

Messinggehäuse vernickelt, Vereila oder Burgunderrot
Weißes Zifferblatt. Gewölbtes Glas
1 Tag Repetierwecker auf Rückwandglocke

Brass case nickeled, Vereila or Burgundy
White dial. Convex glass
1 day repeat alarm on bell at back

Boîte laiton nickelée, Vereila ou rouge Bourgogne
Cadran blanc. Verre bombée
30 heures réveil à répétition sur timbre au fond

Caja de latón niquelada, Vereila ó Borgoña
Esfera blanca. Vidrio convexo
1 dia de despertador con repetición sobre campana atrás

Großes Werk No. 10 – Large movement No. 10 · Grand mouvement No. 10 · Máquina grande No. 10

LARGO No. 9038 Rep.

17 cm — 6³/₄ inches.

Metallgehäuse vernickelt oder Messinggehäuse Vereila oder Burgunderrot
Weißes Zifferblatt
1 Tag Repetier- und Dauerwecker auf Rückwandglocke

Metal case nickeled or brass case Vereila or Burgundy
White dial
1 day repeat and continuous alarm on bell at back

Boîte métal nickelée ou laiton Vereila ou rouge Bourgogne
Cadran blanc
30 heures réveil à répétition et continuelle sur timbre au fond

Caja de metal niquelada ó latón color Vereila ó Borgoña
Esfera blanca
1 dia de despertador con repetición y continuo. Campana atrás

HIPPO BELL REPEATER No. 9055

12,5 cm — 5 inches.

Metallgehäuse blau oder rotbraun lackiert oder Chrom
Weißes Zifferblatt
1 Tag Repetierwecker auf Innenglocke (Werk No. 231)

Metal case lacquered blue or redbrown or chrome case
White dial
1 day repeat alarm on bell inside the case (Movt. No. 231)

Boîte métal laquée bleu ou brun-rouge ou chromée
Cadran blanc
30 heures réveil à répétition, sonnerie sur cloche (Mouvt. No. 231)

Caja de metal pintada azul ó castaño ó cromada
Esfera blanca
1 dia de despertador con repetición sobre campana (Máq. No. 231)

Plate 79
Cat.year
1930

ROMEO
No. 174

8¼ cm = 3¼, inches

Messinggehäuse vernickelt,
verkupfert, Verelfa, Brillantschwarz
oder Burgunderrot
Bombiertes Glas
1 Tag Gehwerk

Brass case nickelled or coppered
Verelfa, Brilliant black or Burgundy
Convex glass
1 day lever time

Boîte laiton nickelé, cuivré
Verelfa, Noir brillant ou Rouge Bourgogne
Verre bombé
30 heures simple ancre

Caja de latón niquelado ó cobrizado
Verelfa, Negro brillante ó Borgoña
Vidrio bombado
1 dia simple á áncora

ROMEO
No. 174½

10 cm = 4 inches

Messinggehäuse vernickelt,
verkupfert, Verelfa, Brillantschwarz
oder Burgunderrot
Bombiertes Glas
1 Tag Wecker

Brass case nickelled or coppered
Verelfa, Brilliant black or Burgundy
Convex glass
1 day alarm

Boîte laiton nickelé, cuivré
Verelfa, Noir brillant ou Rouge Bourgogne
Verre bombé
30 heures ou Rouge réveil

Caja de latón niquelado ó cobrizado
Verelfa, Negro brillante ó Borgoña
Vidrio bombado
1 dia de despertador

TIP-TOP III
No. 121½

8½ cm = 3¼, inches

Messinggehäuse vernickelt, verkupfert, Verelfa, Brillantschwarz
oder Burgunderrot
Weißes Email-Zifferblatt Bombiertes Facettenglas
1 Tag Wecker

Brass case nickelled, coppered, Verelfa, Brilliant black or Burgundy
White enamel dial
Convex bevelled glass
1 day alarm

Boîte laiton nickelé, cuivré, Verelfa, Noir brillant ou Rouge Bourgogne
Cadran émail blanc
Verre bombé à biseau
30 heures à réveil

Caja de latón, niquelado, cobrizado, Verelfa, Negro brillante ó Borgoña
Esfera blanca esmaltada
Vidrio bombado y biselado
1 dia de despertador

TIP-TOP IV
No. 122½

7 cm = 2¾, inches

Mit oder ohne Radium-Blatt — With or without Radium dial — Avec ou sans cadran Radium — Con ó sin esfera luminosa

Plate 80
Cat.# D18
Year 1929

125

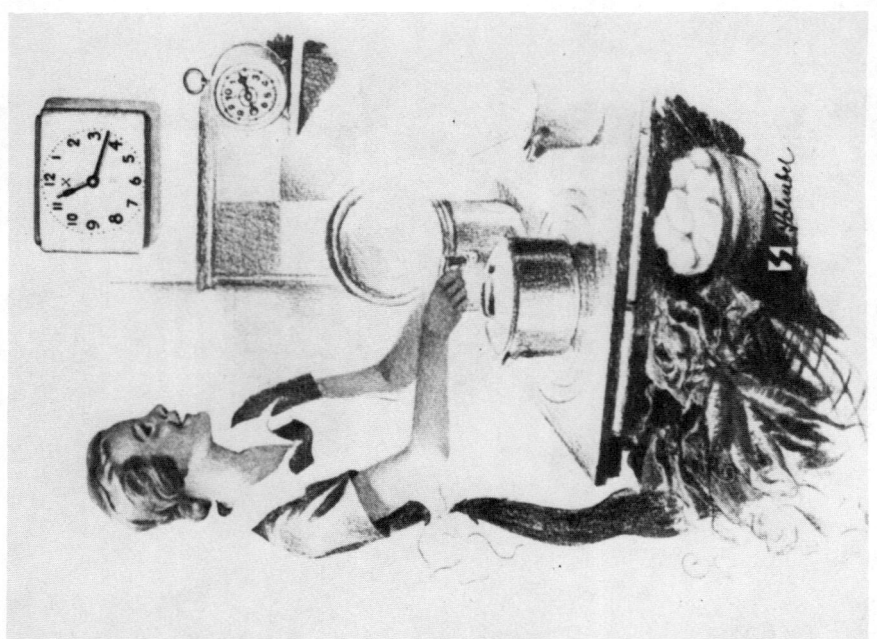

Uhren für Küche und Kinderzimmer

Kitchen- and Nursery Clocks

Pendules pour cuisine et nursery

Relojes para cocinas y piezas de niños

Plate 81
Cat.#31
Year 1930

126

Küchenuhren in Schleiflackgehäusen, Bürouhren

KITCHEN CLOCKS in LAQUER CASE

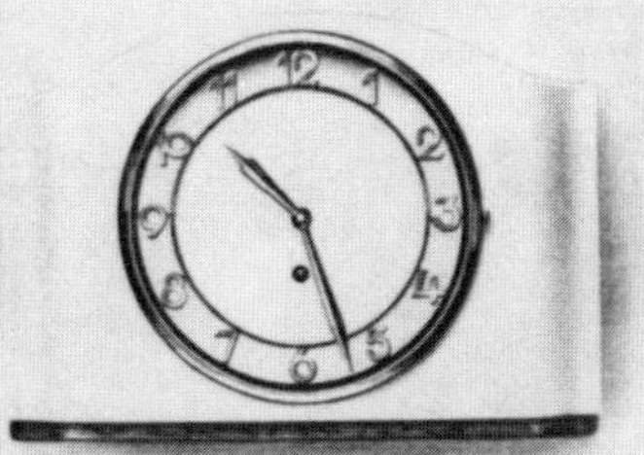

018 394 20,5 · 29,5 cm

All 14 day movement

Alle Gehwerke 14 Tage

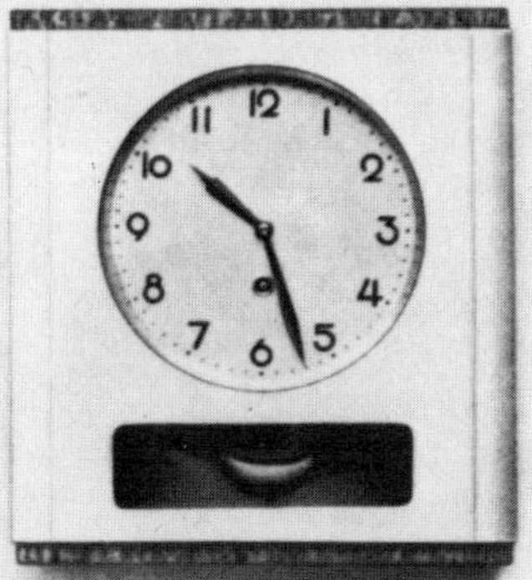

018 377, 018 432 30,5 × 28,5 cm

018 394
Elfenbein mit echt Birke (wandanliegend)
Chromausstattung
8 Tag Ankergehwerk Nr. 246

036 18 394
Synchron-Gehwerk
Ladenpreis **RM. 25.—**

018 377
14 Tag Schlagwerk Bim Bam

018 432
14 Tag Pendelgehwerk
Elfenbeinmattlack mit Birke poliert
7" Elfenbeinlackblatt

018 360
Nußbaumfarbig, Türe Nußbaum poliert
Zweifarbiges Silberblatt 25 × 27 cm
8 Tag Ankergehwerk Nr. 246

036 18 360
Synchron-Gehwerk
Ladenpreis **RM. 29.50**

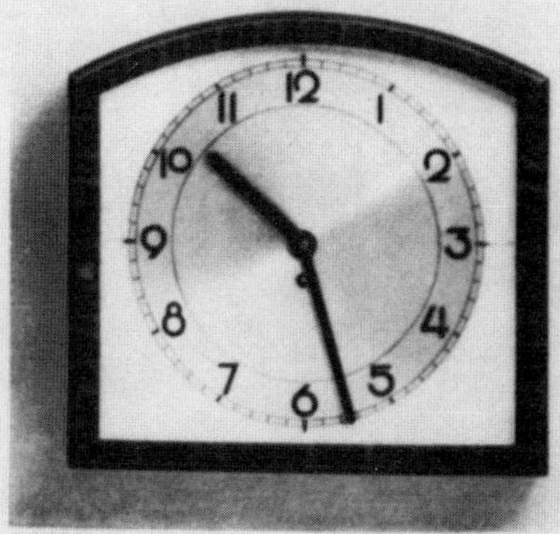

018 360 30 × 32 cm

Plate 82
Cat.year
1930

Steingut-Teller — Stone ware plates — Assiettes faïence — Platos de loza

No. 6101

Delft-Verzierung
Delft decoration — Décor Delft
Decoración Delft

1 Tag Anker- oder 8 Tag Pendelgehwerk
1 day lever time or 8 day pendulum time
30 heures simple ancre ou 8 jours simple à balancier
1 dia simple à áncora ó 8 dias simple à pendola

No. 6129

Weiß mit Schwarz
White with black — Blanc et noir
Blanco y negro

1 Tag oder 8 Tag Anker-Gehwerk. 8 Tag Pendel-Gehwerk
1 day or 8 day lever time. 8 day pendulum time
1 our ou 8 jours simple ancre. 8 jours simple à balancier
1 dia ó 8 dias simple à áncora. 8 dias simple à pendola

No. 6102

Weiß mit Goldlinien
White with gilt lines — Blanc avec lignes or
Blanco y oro

1 Tag Anker- oder 8 Tag Pendelgehwerk
1 day lever time or 8 day pendulum time
30 heures simple ancre ou 8 jours simple à balancier
1 dia simple à áncora ó 8 dias simple à pendola

21 cm = 8¼ inches

No. 6104

20½ cm = 11⅛ inches
Delft-Verzierung — Décor Delft
Delft decoration — Decoración Delft

8 oder 14 Tag Pendel-Gehwerk — 8 or 14 day
pendulum time — 8 ou 15 jours simple à
balancier — 8 ó 15 dias simple à pendola

No. 6130

25 x 25 cm = 10 x 10 inches
Weiß mit Blumen
White with flowers — Blanc avec des fleurs
Blanco con flores

1 Tag Anker-Gehwerk — 1 day lever time
30 heures simple ancre — 1 dia simple à áncora
1 jour simple ancre ou à balancier

No. 6126

22 x 22 cm = 2⅞ x 2⅞ inches
Décor Delft

No. 6127

25 x 25 cm = 10 x 10 inches
Delft-Verzierung
Delft decoration — Decoración Delft

8 Tag Anker- oder Pendel-Gehwerk — 8 day lever time or pendulum time —
8 dias simple à áncora ó à pendola

Plate 83
Cat.#D18
Year 1929

128

Studio-Uhren

Wecker in Metall- und Holzgehäusen

Studio Clocks · Alarm Clocks in metal and wooden cases

Réveils „Studio" · Réveils en boîtes métal et bois

Relojes de Estudio · Despertadores en cajas de metal y madera

Plate 84
Cat.year
1930

129

Plate 85
Cat.#D18
Year 1929

130

Plate 86
-Alarm clock with music   Junghans
  works-   Archive

  "1269"The BLEY index No.(Ref.page 86"BLEY")

Plate 86A
-Alarm clock with music   Junghans
 works-   Archive
  "T"=Time windup "A"=Alarm windup

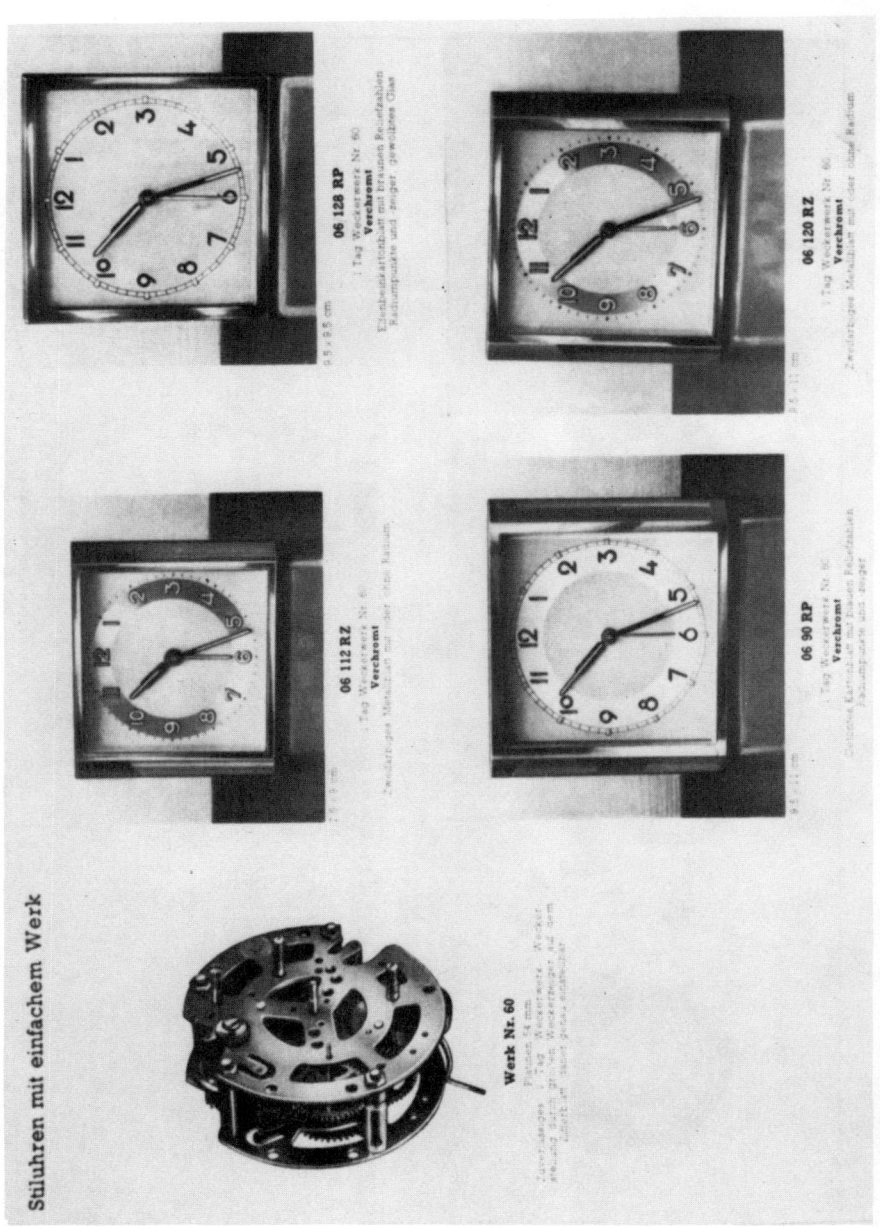

Stuhren mit einfachem Werk

06 128 RP
1 Tag Weckerwerk Nr 60
Verchromt
Einbruchssicherheit mit blauem Feuerbahlen
Radiumquarte und zeiger gewölbtes Glas

06 120 RZ
1 Tag Weckerwerk Nr 60
Verchromt
Zweifarbiges Metalblatt mit oder ohne Radium

06 112 RZ
1 Tag Weckerwerk Nr 60
Verchromt
Zweifarbiges Metalblatt mit oder ohne Radium

06 90 RP
1 Tag Weckerwerk Nr 60
Verchromt
Getöntes Kartonblatt mit blauem Feuerbahlen
Radiumquarte und zeiger

Werk Nr. 60
Format 54 mm.
1 Tag Weckerwerk, Wecker
und Zeiger grösse, exaktuhren

Plate 87
 Cat.#31
Year 1930

133

No. 2395	No. 2396	No. 2397	No. 2398
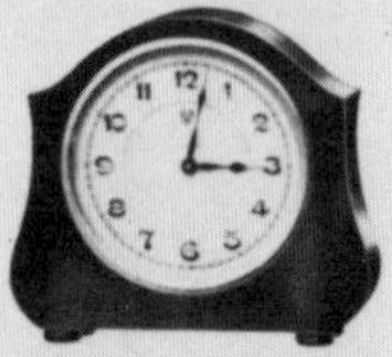	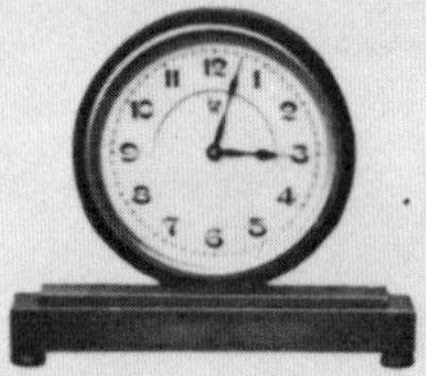	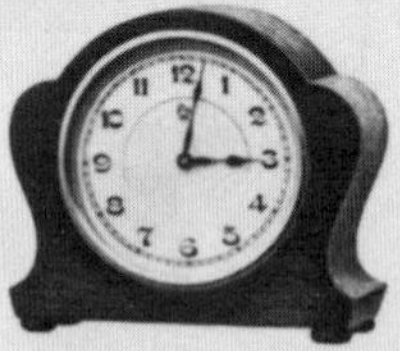	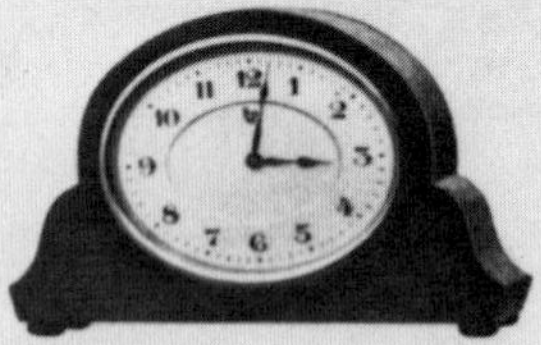
10,5×11,5 cm = 4¼×4½ inches	11,5×13 cm = 4½×5¼ inches	10,5×11,5 cm = 4¼×4½ inches	10,5×16 cm = 4¼×6¼ inches
Holzgehäuse **blau, grün oder rot lackiert** Weißes, geglänztes Zifferblatt Mattgold-Lünette Gewölbtes Glas	**Holzgehäuse** **blau, grün oder rot lackiert** Weißes, geglänztes Zifferblatt Mattgold-Lünette Gewölbtes Glas	**Eiche** Weißes, geglänztes Zifferblatt Mattgold-Lünette Gewölbtes Glas	**Eiche** Weißes, geglänztes Zifferblatt Mattgold-Lünette Gewölbtes Glas
Lacquered wood case **blue, red or green** White glaced dial Dull gilt bezel Convex glass	**Lacquered wood case** **blue, red or green** White glaced dial Dull gilt bezel Convex glass	**Oak** White glaced dial Dull gilt bezel Convex glass	**Oak** White glaced dial Dull gilt bezel Convex glass
Cage bois **laqué bleu, rouge ou vert** Cadran glacé blanc Lunette dorée mat Verre bombé	**Cage bois** **laqué bleu, rouge ou vert** Cadran glacé blanc Lunette dorée mat Verre bombé	**Chêne** Cadran glacé blanc Lunette dorée mat Verre bombé	**Chêne** Cadran glacé blanc Lunette dorée mat Verre bombé
Caja de madera **pintada verde azul ó colorado** Esfera blanca Bisel dorado mate Vidrio convexo	**Caja de madera** **pintada verde azul ó colorado** Esfera blanca Bisel dorado mate Vidrio convexo	**Roble** Esfera blanca Bisel dorado mate Vidrio convexo	**Roble** Esfera blanca Bisel dorado mate Vidrio Convexo

1 Tag Gehwerk oder Wecker — 1 day time or alarm or 8 day lever time — 30 heures simple ou à réveil — 1 dia simple ó despertador

Mit oder ohne Radium-Blatt — With or without Radium dial — Avec ou sans cadran Radium — Con ó sin esfera luminosa

Plate 88
Cat.#36
Year 1930

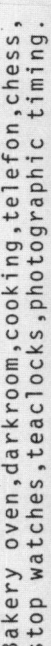

Bakery oven,darkroom,cooking,telefon,chess,
stop watches,teaclocks,photographic timing.

PFEILKREUZ KURZZEITMESSER

TIMER of ALL TYPES

Seit mehr als 40 Jahren im Handel als:

Backwächter, Badeuhren, Belichtungsuhren, Bestrahlungsuhren, Billarduhren,
Blitzturnieruhren, Dunkelkammeruhren, Eieruhren, Eindünstuhren, Fern-
sprechuhren, Schachuhren, Sekundenzähler, Stoppuhren, Teeuhren, Zeitmerker

Bitte verlangen Sie Musterbuch K 6 über Pfeilkreuz-Kurzzeitmesser

Plate 89
Cat.#36
Year 1930

135

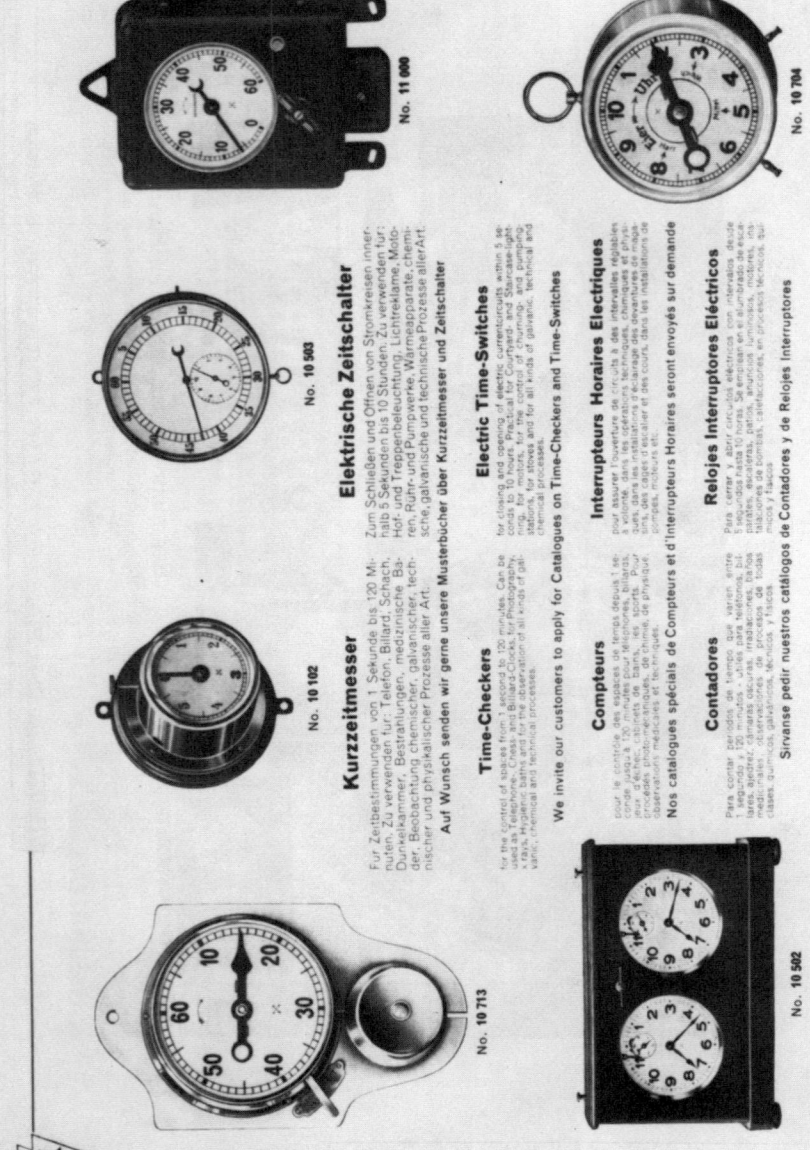

Kurzzeitmesser

Für Zeitbestimmungen von 1 Sekunde bis 120 Minuten. Zu verwenden für Telefon, Billard, Schach, Dunkelkammer, Bestrahlungen, medizinische Bäder, Beobachtung chemischer, galvanischer, technischer und physikalischer Prozesse aller Art.

Elektrische Zeitschalter

Zum Schließen und Öffnen von Stromkreisen innerhalb 5 Sekunden bis 10 Stunden. Zu verwenden für: Hub- und Trepperbeleuchtung, Lichtreklame, Motoren, Rühr- und Pumpwerke, Wärmeapparate, chemische, galvanische und technische Prozesse aller Art.

Auf Wunsch senden wir gerne unsere Musterbücher über Kurzzeitmesser und Zeitschalter

Time-Checkers

for the control of spaces from 1 second to 120 minutes. Can be used as Telephone-, Chess for the observation of all kinds of galvanic, chemical and technical processes.

Electric Time-Switches

for closing and opening of electric currentcircuits within 5 seconds to 10 hours. To be used for hoist- and staircase-lighting, for motors, for the control of churning- and pumping stations, for stoves and for all kinds of galvanic, technical and chemical processes.

We invite our customers to apply for Catalogues on Time-Checkers and Time-Switches

Compteurs

pour le contrôle des espaces de temps depuis 1 seconde jusqu'à 120 minutes. Servent pour le Téléphone, pour les jeux d'échecs etc., pour procéder à l'observation de tous les procédés photo-mécaniques, de chimie, de physique, observations médicales et techniques.

Interrupteurs Horaires Electriques

pour assurer l'ouverture de circuits à des intervalles réglables à volonté, dans les opérations techniques, chimiques et physiques, dans les cages d'escalier et des cours, dans les installations de pompes, moteurs etc.

Nos catalogues spéciaux de Compteurs et d'Interrupteurs Horaires seront envoyés sur demande

Contadores

Para contar periodos de tiempo que varian entre 1 segundo y 120 minutos - utiles para telefonos, billares, ajedrez, observaciones de procesos de todas clases, quimicos, galvanicos, tecnicos y fisicos.

Relojes Interruptores Eléctricos

Para cerrar y abrir circuitos eléctricos con intervalos desde 5 seg.-dos hasta 10 horas. Se emplean en el alumbrado de escaleras, anuncios luminosos, en actuaciones de motores, instalaciones de bombas, en procesos técnicos, químicos y físicos.

Sírvanse pedir nuestros catálogos de Contadores y de Relojes Interruptores

No. 11 600
No. 10 704
No. 10 503
No. 10 102
No. 10 713
No. 10 502

Plate 90
Cat. #36
Year 1930

136

ATO 8901

ATO 8910

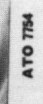

ATO 7754

Elektrische Schwachstrom-Uhr ATO

Trockenelement-Antrieb · Kein Netzanschluß · Einzeluhren · Uhrenanlagen
Verlangen Sie unser Spezialmusterbuch

Electric Weakcurrent Clock ATO

Dry-battery-motion · No plugging to light-socket · Self contained clocks · Installation
of master and secondary clocks · **Apply for our Special-Catalogue**

Horloge à courant faible ATO

Impulsion par pile sèche · Pas d'alimentation par le réseau · Horloges indépendantes
Installation complète d'horloges · **Demandez s. v. pl. catalogue spécial**

Reloj eléctrico ATO

Impulso por pila seca · Sin conexión con la red de alumbrado · Relojes independientes
Combinaciónes de relojes · **Pídase nuestro catálogo especial**

ATO 7923

Plate 91
Cat. #36
Year 1930

137

ATO 7753 Einzeluhr

ATO SINGLE Clock
Second escapement
movement

ATO 7754 Einzeluhr

ATO SINGLE CLOCK
Second escapement
movement

Plate 92
Cat.#36
Year 1930

ATO-Signaluhr als Einzeluhr und Hauptuhr

ATO-SIGNAL CLOCK as SINGLE CLOCK and MASTER CLOCK

Signalvorrichtung bei der ATO-Signaluhr 8010

Signal release of
the ATO-SIGNAL Clock
8010

ATO 8010 Einzeluhr
ATO H 8010 Hauptuhr

52.5 · 37 · 9.5 cm

ATO 8010 SINGLE Clock
ATO H 8010 Master Clock
Oak case

ATO-Werk

ATO-Movement

Plate 93
Cat.#36
Year 1930

139

MANTLE - CLOCKS

**PFEILKREUZ-
TISCHUHREN**

Pfeilkreuz-Uhren [X]

Plate 94
Cat#32
Year 1935
-1936

Nr. 3707

22 × 43 cm

Mahagoni poliert

Silber-Skelettzahlenreif, 18 cm Chromäanette, Chromfüße

Mahagony polished
Silver sceleton
chapter ring.

Nr. 3703

22 × 43 cm

Kirschbaum poliert

Silberzahlenreif mit aufgelegten Chromzahlen

Cherry-polished
Silver plated chapter
ring with brass-chrom
plated numbers.

Halbstund-Rechenschlag auf Parsifalgong (Bim-Bam) mit *Schlagebehälter* oder ¼ Westminsterschlag

Half-hour rack strike system-PARSIFAL GONG(Bim-Bam)
with strike silencer or 4/4 Westminster strike.

Plate 95
Cat.#32
Year 1935-
       1936

Oak carved Walnut-polished
case.Silver sceleton chapter
ring.Half hour rack strike
system,PARSIFAL GONG (Bim-Bam)
or 4/4 Westminster strike.

Nr. 3691

20.5 18 cm

Eiche geschnitzt mit geflammt Nußbaum poliert
Silber-Skelettzahlenreif. 16 cm Chromlünette

Halbstund-Rechenschlag auf Parsifalgong (Bim-Bam) oder ⁴, Westminsterschlag

Nr. 3692

20.5 18 cm

Eiche geschnitzt mit geflammt Nußbaum poliert
Silber-Skelettzahlenreif. 26 cm Chromlünette

same as model 3691

Nr. 3693

21 36 cm

Eiche mit geflammt Nußbaum poliert
Silber-Skelettzahlenreif. 17 cm Chromlünette

same as model 3691

Plate 96
Cat.#32
Year 1935
     -1936

142

68 × 27 cm ~ 26¾ × 10½ inches

021/12

Auch mit Adleraufsatz lieferbar
Also with eagle instead of horse
Livrable aussi avec aigle au lieu du cheval
Se suministra también con aderezo de águila

89.5 × 35 cm ~ 34½ × 13¾ inches

021/32

Walnut polished,14 day half
and full hr.strike movement,
hight= 26 3/4" x 10 1/2"

Plate 97
Cat.#31
Year 1930

143

MINIATURE - WALL REGULATOR -- KLEIN WANDUHREN

No. 19 URNE URN
No. 20 ADLER EAGLE
No. 21 PFERD HORSE

No. 2819 URNE URN
No. 2820 ADLER EAGLE

No. 2821
PFERD HORSE

No. 119 URNE URN
No. 120 ADLER EAGLE
No. 121 PFERD HORSE

Walnut,
part polished
1 day strike
movement.
68 cm long
Nussbaum,teil-
weise poliert.
1 Tag Schlagwerk

Walnut,
part polished,
glass on sides,
14 day strike
movement.
Nussbaum,teil-
weise poliert.
14 Tag Schlagwerk,
Glasseiten.

Walnut,
part polished
1 day or 14 day
strike movement.
77 cm long
Nussbaum,teil-
weise poliert.
1 Tag oder 14
Tag Schlagwerk.

Plate 98
Cat.#D18
Year 1929

144

No.783 Urn -Urne
784 Horse-Pferd
786 Eagle-Adler

No.821 Urn -Urne
822 Eagle-Adler
823 Horse-Pferd

No. 783

No. 786

Walnut,14 day movement,half hour strike spiral gong.

Walnuss,14 Tag Gehwerk,Halbstund-Schlagwerk auf Tonfeder.

Plate 99
Cat.#D18
Year 1929

145

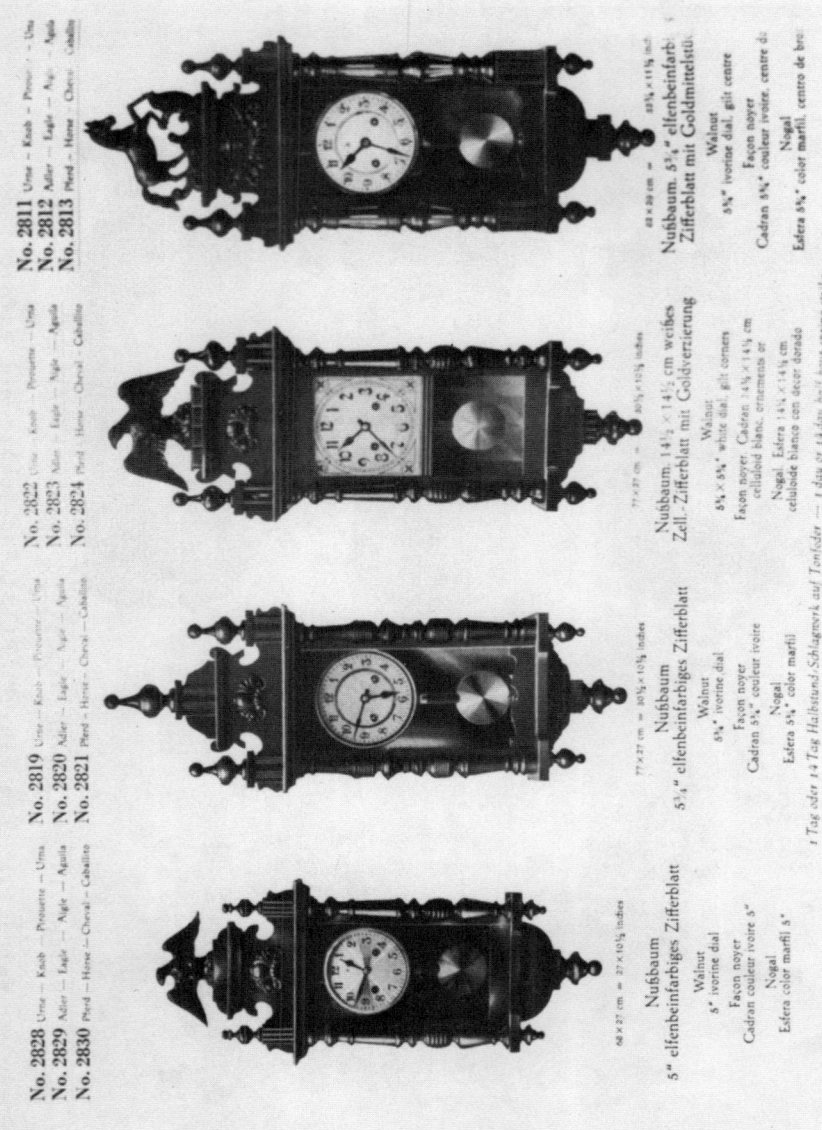

No. 2828 Urna – Knob – Primavera – Urna
No. 2829 Adler – Eagle – Aigle – Agula
No. 2830 Pferd – Horse – Cheval – Caballito

No. 2819 Urna – Knob – Primavera – Urna
No. 2820 Adler – Eagle – Aigle – Agula
No. 2821 Pferd – Horse – Cheval – Caballito

No. 2822 Urna – Knob – Primavera – Urna
No. 2823 Adler – Eagle – Aigle – Agula
No. 2824 Pferd – Horse – Cheval – Caballito

No. 2811 Urna – Knob – Primer – – Urna
No. 2812 Adler – Eagle – Aigle – Agula
No. 2813 Pferd – Horse – Cheval – Caballito

68 × 27 cm = 27 × 10½ inches

Nußbaum
5" elfenbeinfarbiges Zifferblatt

Walnut
5" ivorine dial

Façon noyer
Cadran couleur ivoire 5"

Nogal
Esfera color marfil 5"

77 × 27 cm = 30⅜ × 10½ inches

Nußbaum
5¾" elfenbeinfarbiges Zifferblatt

Walnut
5¾" ivorine dial

Façon noyer
Cadran 5¾" couleur ivoire

Nogal
Esfera 5¾" color marfil

77 × 37 cm = 30½ × 10½ inches

Nußbaum, 14½ × 14½ cm weißes
Zell.-Zifferblatt mit Goldverzierung

Walnut
5¾ × 5¾" white dial, gilt corners

Façon noyer Cadran 14¾ × 14¾ cm
celluloid blanc, ornaments de

Nogal Esfera 14¾ × 14¾ cm
celuloide blanco con decor dorado

68 × 89 cm = 33¾ × 11¾ inch

Nußbaum, 5¾" elfenbeinfarbi
Zifferblatt mit Goldmittelstü

Walnut
5¾" ivorine dial, gilt centre

Façon noyer
Cadran 5¾" couleur ivoire, centre d:

Nogal
Esfera 5¾" color marfil, centro de bro

1 Tag oder 14 Tag Halbstund Schlagwerk auf Tonfeder – 1 day or 14 day half hour spring strike
1 jour ou 15 jours sonnerie heure et demie sur ressort timbre – 1 dia ó 15 dias sonería hora y media sobre resorte

Plate 100
Cat.# 31
Year 1930

146

GRUPPE 023

WALL CLOCKS -- WANDUHREN

54,5 × 25,5 cm — 21 ½ × 10 inches

023 88

Eiche - Oak - Chêne - Roble

54,5 × 25,5 cm — 21 ½ × 10 inches

023 90

Eiche - Oak - Chêne - Roble

54,5 × 25,5 cm — 21 ½ × 10 inches

023 92

Eiche - Oak - Chêne - Roble

14 day 1/2 hour strike,plain strike-Rod gong BIM-BAM

Metal dial

In all shades of oak colour.

14 Tag Halbstund-Schlagwerk,Tonfeder-Stabgong BIM-BAM

Metallblatt

In allen Eichenfarben lieferbar.

Plate 101
Cat.# 31
@ Year 1929

147

63.5 × 33.5 cm – 25 × 13½ inches	63.5 × 33.5 cm – 25 × 13½ inches	63.5 × 33.5 cm – 25 × 13½ inches
024 214	**024 215**	**024 216**
Eiche – Oak – Chêne – Roble	**Eiche** – Oak – Chêne – Roble	**Eiche** – Oak – Chêne – Roble

WALL CLOCKS -- WANDUHREN

14 day 1/2 hour strike,plain strike-Rod gong BIM-BAM

Metal dial

In all shades of oak colour.

14 Tag Halbstund-Schlagwerk,Tonfeder-Stabgong BIM-BAM

Metallblatt

In allen Eichenfarben lieferbar.

Plate 102
Cat.# 31
Year 1930

Exerpts from the *"DEUTSCHE UHRMACHER ZEITUNG"* No.18,1901:

EDUARD HAUSER,Founder of the LENZKIRCH Clock Factory,

LENZKIRCH,Black Forest

By Prof.F.Anton Hubbuch,Strassbourg-
Elsac-Lorrain,August 31.1901

"In addition to the large responsibility for the LENZKIRCH
enterprise Hauser always found enough time for his family.
To provide a solidly founded education for his childern
was his main goal.His oldest son was very much an artisan
craftsman,and designed for the last thirty years the cases
of the LENZKIRCH clocks.His second son Carl August,born
September 24,1854 was a watchmaker appreticed to the very
well known Master Watchmaker Martens in Freiburg,Black
Forest.His youngest son Emil was a tool and die designer.
But proposed plans with his sons did not materialise.
After Hauser took an early retirement and let his sons run
the LENZKIRCH enterprise,Carl August quit his father's
company,soon followed by his brother Emil and both have
been employed since about 1900 with the HAMBURG-AMERICAN
Clock Company in Schramberg.
Carl August's experience in the precision-clockmaking
had an immense influence on the "AMERICAN SYSTEM"and will
certainly increase the good reputation the "HAMBURG
AMERICAN Clock Co."has on the domestic and worldwide market"

Hennig Archive

* *German Watchmaker Journal*

Wer sich anschickt, eine Gründungs- bezw. Entwickelungsgeschichte der in Rede stehenden Fabrik schreiben zu wollen, kann dies am besten dadurch vollbringen, daß er die Lebensgeschichte desjenigen Mannes hierher setzt, der diese Fabrik gegründet hat, dessen geistiges Gepräge dieselbe heute noch trägt, und der gerade während dieses halben Jahrhunderts der Entwickelung seiner Gründung mit Leib und Seele zugethan war. Wer von den deutschen Uhrmachern kannte ihn nicht, jenen lebhaften Kämpen der Uhrmacherkunst, an dem Alles zuckte, wenn er von seinen mit soviel Scharfsinn erdachten Maschinen, wenn er von den Studien auf seinen Reisen erzählen konnte! Und wie blitzte sein scharfes Auge, wenn seine Gedanken dabei verwilten, wie das Geschene in der eigenen Branche nutzbare Verwendung finden könnte! Eduard Hauser war aber weit über die Grenzen unseres Vaterlandes hinaus bekannt als genialer Konstrukteur, und mancher Ausruf der Bewunderung wurde dem aus fernen Landen herübergekommenen Kunden und Geschäftsfreunde entlockt, wenn er in das geheime Getriebe jener Fabrik einen Blick werfen durfte, der ihm verrieth, daß hier in origineller Durchbildung die komplizirte Fabrikation wie am Schnürchen durch eine unzählige Reihe von Spezialmaschinen durchgeführt wird.

An seiner Wiege hat man wohl nicht daran gedacht, daß der muntere Knabe späterhin einen so hervorragenden Antheil an der Hebung der sozialen Lage einer ganzen Gegend durch Einführung eines neuen Industriezweiges nehmen würde. Geboren am 21. August 1825 als Sohn eines Lehrers in Rothweil am Kaiserstuhl — einem Weinbau treibenden Gebirgsdörfchen —, genoß er seine Erziehung zunächst im elterlichen Hause und besuchte sodann die Lateinschule im benachbarten Altbreisach; denn schon frühzeitig erkannte man seine geistigen

hoher Blüthe stand und gute Werkzeugmacher in allen uhrmachenden Orten zu finden waren. Die Jahre 1846/47 brachte Hauser in verschiedenen Werkstätten der Werkzeugbranche zu; er lernte, was dort für die Erreichung des Zieles zu holen war, und kehrte nach dem Schwarzwalde zurück, um eine eigene Werkstätte zur Herstellung von Werkzeugen und Maschinen für die Uhrmacherei einzurichten. Daneben befaßte er sich mit dem Plane, Bestandtheile für massive Uhren für die hausindustriellen Uhrmacher zu fertigen, damit dieselben in die Lage versetzt würden, mit solchen Uhren gegen Frankreich und England konkurrenzfähig zu werden.

Die Hauser'schen Werkzeuge verschafften sich auf dem Schwarzwalde bald einen Ruf, und H. hatte die Genugthuung, daß er bei Einrichtung der ersten Uhrmacherschule in Furtwangen im Jahre 1850 Muster - Werkzeuge liefern durfte. Seinen Lieblingsplan, die Massivuhrmacherei auf dem Schwarzwalde in weitgehendem Maße einzuführen, konnte er aber nur langsam zur Reife bringen, denn in so kurzer Zeit kann eine alteingesessene Industrie nicht umgestaltet werden. Seine Geduld mit den alten Holzuhrmachern war zu Ende, und so entschloß er sich im Mai 1850 im Verein mit seinem Freunde Ignatz Schöpperle, dem Sohne seines Lehrmeisters, eine Rohwerkfabrik einzurichten, in welcher die Rohwerke für massive Uhren durch Spezialmaschinen soweit vorgearbeitet wurden, daß dem Uhrmacher nur noch die Bearbeitung der Hemmung und das Finiren verblieb. Er verfolgte damit denselben Zweck, wie die damals unter Gerwig's Leitung stehende Uhrmacherschule in Furtwangen, nur schwebte ihm von der Schweiz her ein bewährtes Vorbild vor, sodaß er vielfach berathend in diese Entwickelung eingreifen konnte und in Verbindung mit ihm auch die Normaluhren.

EDUARD HAUSER
geboren 21. August 1825, gestorben 22. Juli 1900

77 × 36 cm — 30¼ × 14⅛ inches   77 × 36 cm — 30¼ × 14⅛ inches

025/559   **025/561**

Polished walnut case   Polished walnut case

Waldgong - Bachgong - 4/4 Westminster strike

Plate 105
Cat.#31
Year 1930

150

GRUPPE 025
Wanduhren
Wall clocks – Régulateurs – Reguladores

78 × 34.5 cm = 30³⁄₄ × 13½ inches   78 × 34.5 cm = 30³⁄₄ × 13½ inches   78 × 33 cm = 30³⁄₄ × 13 inches

025/564

Eiche – Oak – Chêne – Roble

Metallblatt – Metal dial – Cadran métal – Esfera de metal
21.5 cm = 8½ inches

025/566

Eiche – Oak – Chêne – Roble

025/492

Eiche – Oak – Chêne – Roble

025/493

Nußbaum – Walnut – Noyer – Nogal

Metallblatt – Metal dial – Cadran métal – Esfera de metal
20.5 cm = 8 inches

Waldgong – Bachgong – ⁴⁄, Westminsterschlag
Waldgong – Gong „Bim Bam" – ⁴⁄, Westminster chime
Waldgong – Gong „Bim Bam" – ⁴⁄, Carillon Westminster
Soneria sobre Waldgong – Gong „Bim Bam" – ⁴⁄, Carillon Westminster

Eichengehäuse in allen Eichenfarben lieferbar – Oak cases can be had in all oak colours
Les cages chêne se livrent en toutes teintes de chêne – Se hacen las cajas en todos los colores de roble

Plate 105
Cat.#31
Year 1930

G R U P P E 0 2 7

GROUP 027 – MODERN WALL CLOCKS
GRUPPE 027 – MODERNE WANDUHREN

027 62
50 × 28 cm

027 63
50 × 28 cm

027 64
50 × 28 cm

027 55
49.5 × 30 cm

Oak

Caucasian walnut
polished
silver plated
dial,bevelled
glass

Caucasian walnut
polished
silver plated
dial,bevelled
glass

Caucasian walnut
polished
silver plated
dial,bevelled
glass

Caucasian walnut
polished
silver plated
dial,bevelled
glass

Plate 106
Cat.#36

152

GRUPPE 027

Aparte Wanduhren für die moderne Wohnung

Smart wall clocks for the modern home – Pendules art nouveau pour intérieurs modernes
Relojes de pared especiales para la casa moderna

61,5 × 36 cm — 24¼ × 14¼ inches

027/67

**Kaukasisch Nußbaum poliert
Silberblatt, Chromverglasung**

Polished Caucasian walnut
Silver dial, chromium fitting

Noyer Caucasien poli
Cadran argenté, vitrage chromé

Nogal Caúcaso pulido
Esfera plateada, vitraux cromados

61,5 × 36 cm — 24¼ × 14¼ inches

027/68

**Kaukasisch Nußbaum poliert
Silberblatt, Chromauflagen,
Chromverglasung**

Polished Caucasian walnut
Silver dial, chromium ornaments,
chromium fitting

Noyer Caucasien poli
Cadran argenté, applications chromées,
vitrage chromé

Nogal Caúcaso pulido
Esfera plateada, aplicaciones cromadas,
vitraux cromados

Waldgong – Bim Bam 5 Stäbe – ⁴/₄ Westminster

Gong – Gong „Bim Bam": 5 rods – ⁴/₄ Westminster chime

Gong rond – Gong „Bim Bam": 5 tiges – ⁴/₄ Carillon Westminster

Gong redondo – Gong „Bim Bam": 5 varillas – ⁴/₄ Carillon Westminster

Plate 107
Cat.#31
Year 1930

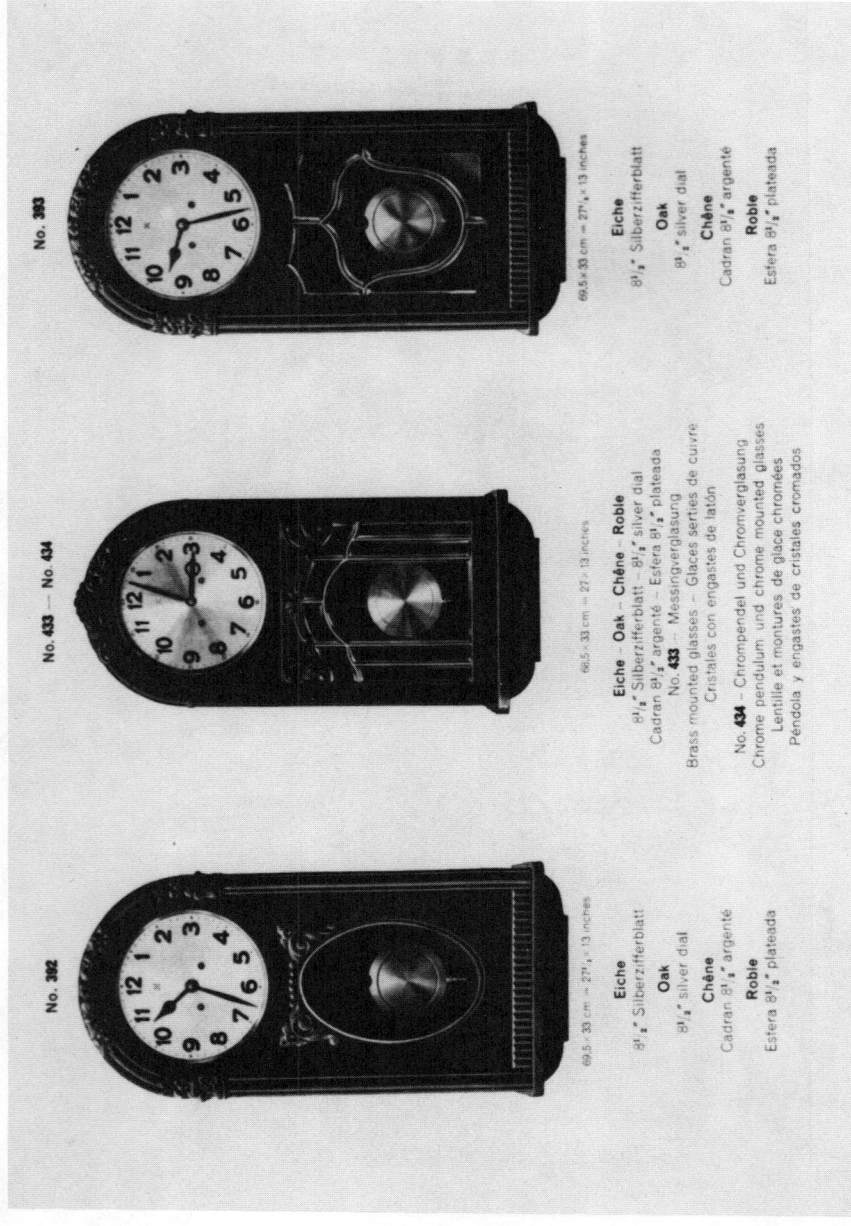

No. 393

69,5×33 cm = 27" × 13 inches

Eiche
8¼" Silberzifferblatt
Oak
8¼" silver dial
Chêne
Cadran 8¼" argenté
Roble
Esfera 8¼" plateada

No. 433 — No. 434

66,5×33 cm = 27×13 inches

Eiche - Oak - Chêne - Roble
8¼" Silberzifferblatt - 8¼" silver dial
Cadran 8¼" argenté - Esfera 8¼" plateada
No. **433** — Messingverglasung
Brass mounted glasses — Glaces serties de cuivre
Cristales con engastes de latón
No. **434** — Chrompendel und Chromverglasung
Chrome pendulum, und chrome mounted glasses
Lentille et montures de glace chromées
Péndola y engastes de cristales cromados

No. 392

69,5×33 cm = 27" × 13 inches

Eiche
8¼" Silberzifferblatt
Oak
8¼" silver dial
Chêne
Cadran 8¼" argenté
Roble
Esfera 8¼" plateada

Plate 108
Cat.#31
Year 1930

154

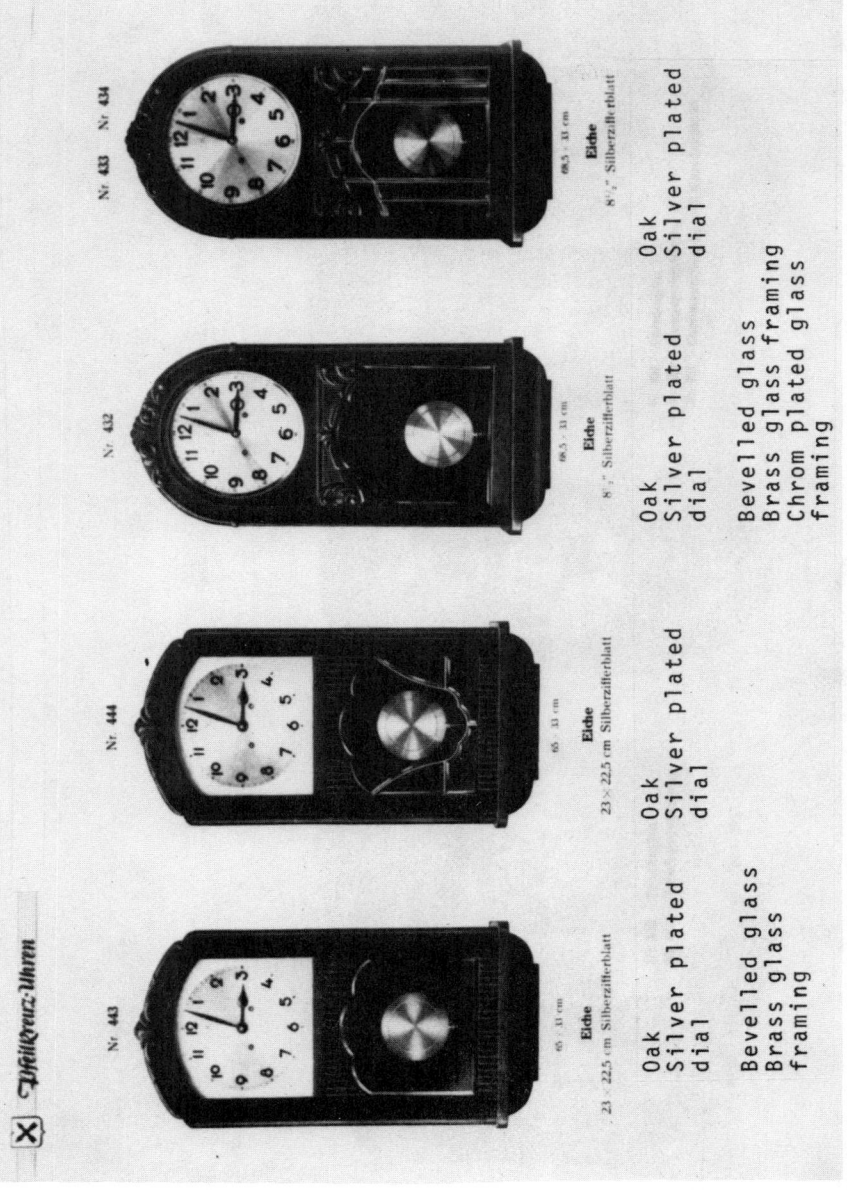

Nr. 433 Nr. 434

Nr. 432

Nr. 444

Nr. 443

Eiche
69,5 × 33 cm Silberzifferblatt

Eiche
69,5 × 33 cm Silberzifferblatt

Eiche
65 × 33 cm
23 × 22,5 cm Silberzifferblatt

Eiche
65 × 33 cm
23 × 22,5 cm Silberzifferblatt

Oak
Silver plated
dial

Bevelled glass
Brass glass framing
Chrom plated glass
framing

Oak
Silver plated
dial

Oak
Silver plated
dial

Bevelled glass
Brass glass
framing

Oak
Silver plated
dial

Bevelled glass
Brass glass
framing

Plate 109
Cat.#36

155

No. 1080

No. 1078   No. 1079

Gewöhnliche Gläser   Facettegläser
Plain glasses   Bevelled glasses
Verres ordinaires   Verres à biseau
Vidrios planos   Vidrios biselados

58 : 27.5 cm = 23 × 11 inches

Eiche oder Nußbaum
6" Silberzifferblatt

Oak or walnut
6" silver dial

Chêne ou noyer
Cadran 6" argenté

Roble ó nogal
Esfera 6" plateada

No. 2626

55 : 29 cm = 21³⁄₄ × 11¹⁄₂ inches

Eiche
7" Silberzifferblatt

Chêne
Cadran 7" argenté

Roble
Esfera 7" plateada

No. 2625

55 : 29 cm = 21³⁄₄ × 11¹⁄₂ inches

Oak
7" silver dial

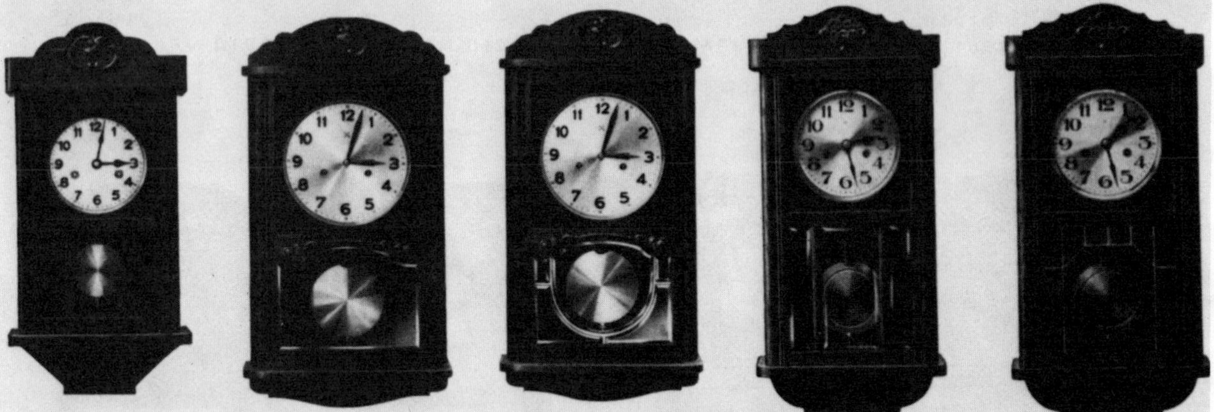

No. 2622

53 : 26 cm = 21 × 10¹⁄₄ inches

Eiche oder Nußbaum
5³⁄₄" Silberzifferblatt

Oak or walnut
5³⁄₄" silver dial

Chêne ou noyer
Cadran 5³⁄₄" argenté

Roble ó nogal
Esfera 5³⁄₄" plateada

Plate 110
Cat.#36

156

Standuhren

Hall Clocks - Horloges de parquet

Relojes de vestíbulo

Plate 111
Cat.#D 22
Year 1929

157

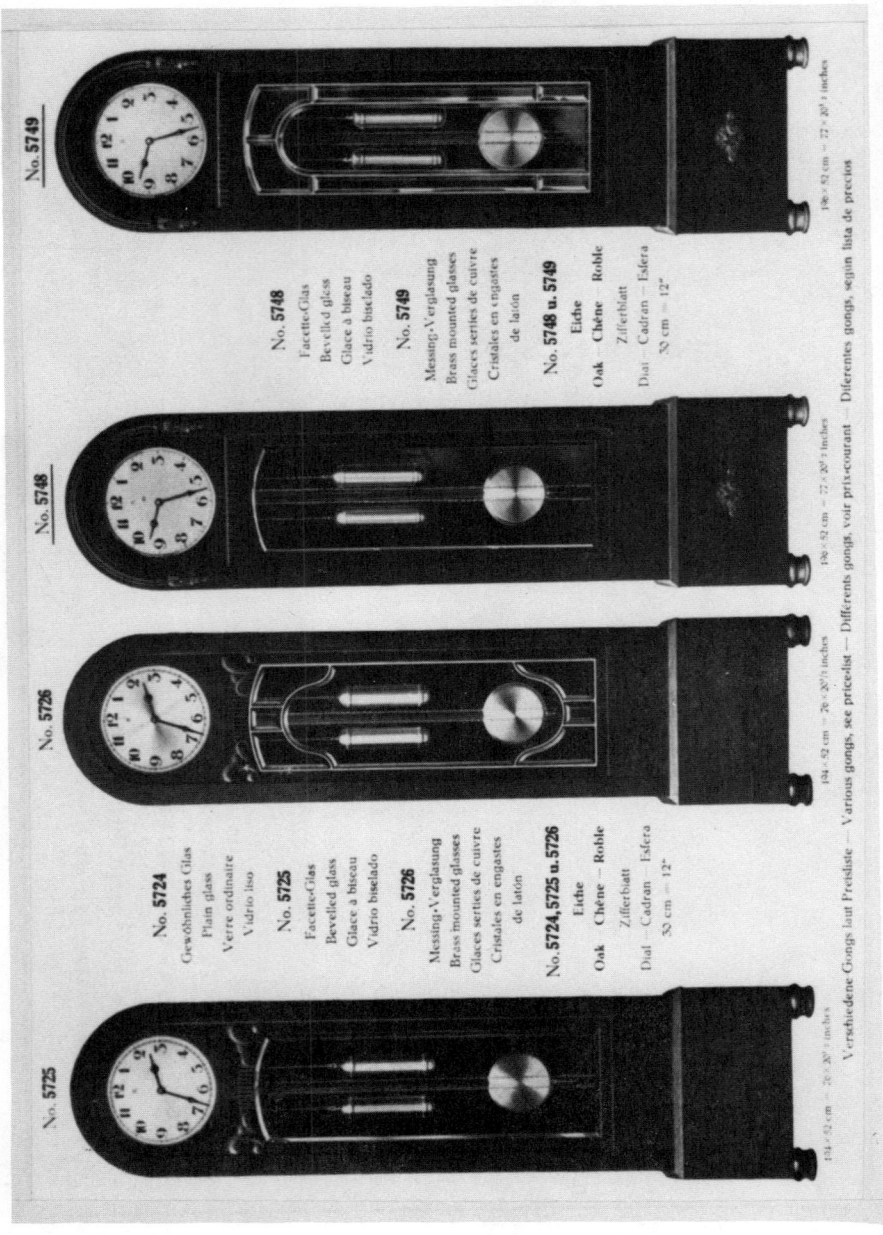

No. 5725

No. 5726

No. 5748

No. 5749

No. 5724
Gewöhnliches Glas
Plain glass
Verre ordinaire
Vidrio liso

No. 5725
Facettte-Glas
Bevelled glass
Glace à biseau
Vidrio biselado

No. 5726
Messing-Verglasung
Brass mounted glasses
Glaces serties de cuivre
Cristales en engastes
de latón

No. 5724, 5725 u. 5726
Eiche
Oak — Chêne — Roble
Zifferblatt
Dial — Cadran — Esfera
30 cm = 12"

No. 5748
Facettte-Glas
Bevelled glass
Glace à biseau
Vidrio biselado

No. 5749
Messing-Verglasung
Brass mounted glasses
Glaces serties de cuivre
Cristales en engastes
de latón

No. 5748 u. 5749
Eiche
Oak — Chêne — Roble
Zifferblatt
Dial — Cadran — Esfera
30 cm = 12"

Verschiedene Gongs laut Preisliste — Various gongs, see pricelist — Différents gongs, voir prix-courant — Differentes gongs, según lista de precios

Plate 112
Cat. #D 22
Year 1929

158

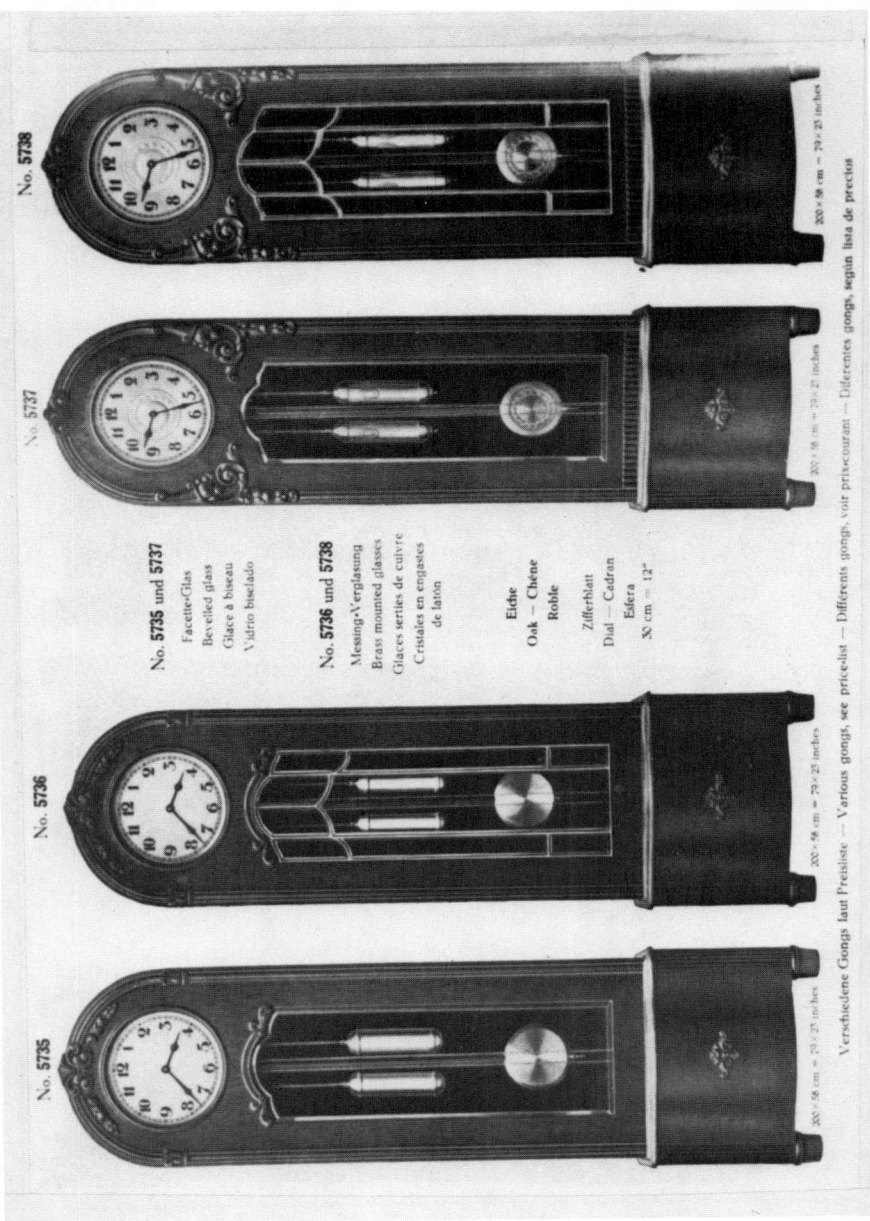

No. 5738

No. 5737

No. 5736

No. 5735

No. 5735 und 5737
Facette-Glas
Beveiled glass
Glace à biseau
Vidrio biselado

No. 5736 und 5738
Messing-Verglasung
Brass mounted glasses
Glaces serties de cuivre
Cristales en engastes
de latón

Eiche
Oak — Chêne
Roble

Zifferblatt
Dial — Cadran
Esfera
30 cm = 12"

200 × 58 cm = 79 × 23 inches

200 × 58 cm = 79 × 23 inches

200 × 58 cm = 79 × 23 inches

200 × 58 cm = 79 × 23 inches

Verschiedene Gongs laut Preisliste — Various gongs, see price-list — Différents gongs, voir prix-courant — Differentes gongs, según lista de precios

Plate 113
Cat. D 22
Year 1929

159

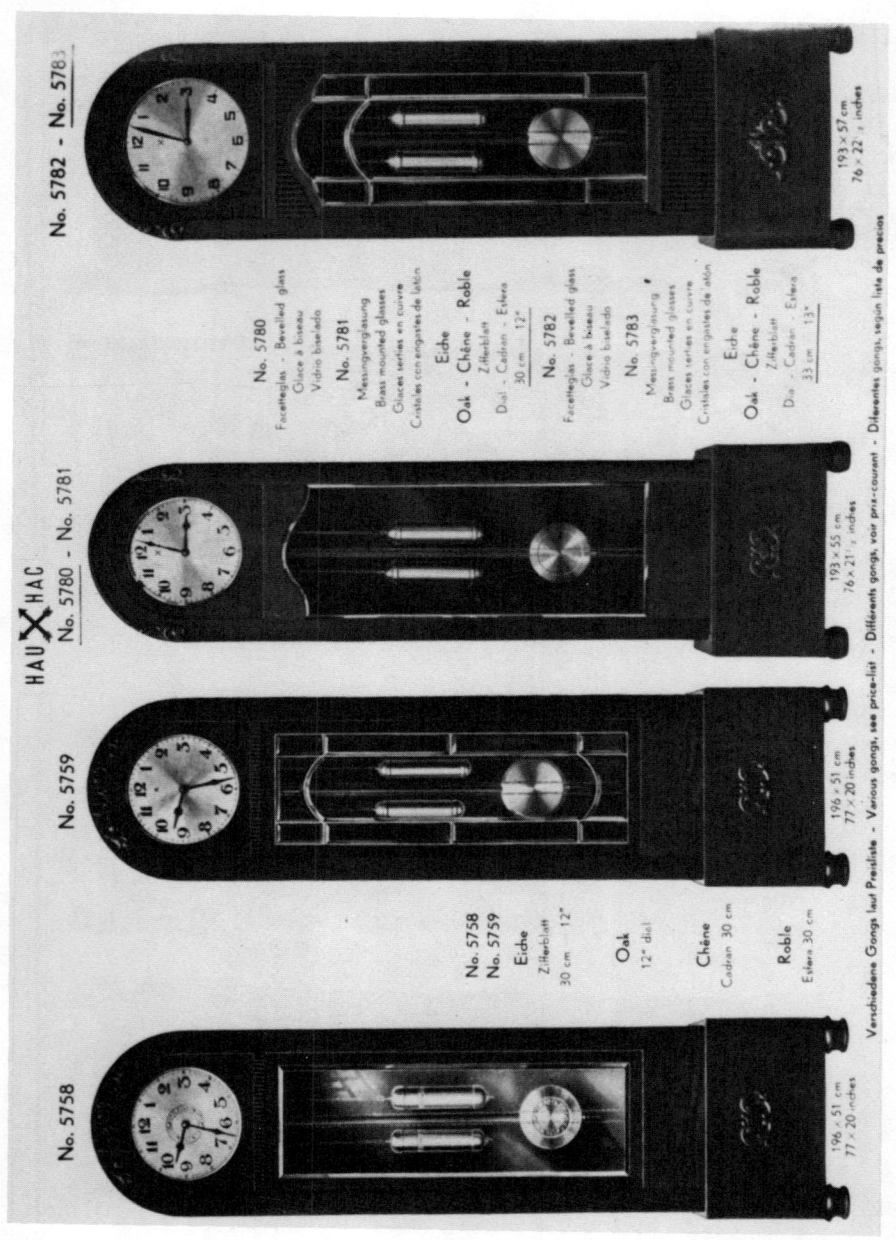

No. 5782 - No. 5783

HAU⨯HAC

No. 5780 - No. 5781

No. 5759

No. 5758

No. 5780
Facetteglas - Bevelled glass
Glace à biseau
Vidrio biselado

No. 5781
Messingverglasung
Brass mounted glasses
Glaces serties en cuivre
Cristales con engastes de latón

Eiche
Oak - Chêne - Roble
Zifferblatt
Dial - Cadran - Esfera
30 cm 12"

No. 5782
Facetteglas - Bevelled glass
Glace à biseau
Vidrio biselado

No. 5783
Messingverglasung
Brass mounted glasses
Glaces serties en cuivre
Cristales con engastes de latón

Eiche
Oak - Chêne - Roble
Zifferblatt
Dial - Cadran - Esfera
33 cm 13"

193 × 57 cm
76 × 22 ½ inches

193 × 55 cm
76 × 21 ½ inches

No. 5758
No. 5759
Eiche
Zifferblatt
30 cm 12"

Oak
12" dial

Chêne
Cadran 30 cm

Roble
Esfera 30 cm

196 × 51 cm
77 × 20 inches

196 × 51 cm
77 × 20 inches

Verschiedene Gongs laut Preisliste - Various gongs, see price-list - Différents gongs, voir prix-courant - Diferentes gongs, según lista de precios

Plate 114
Cat.#31
Year 1930

160

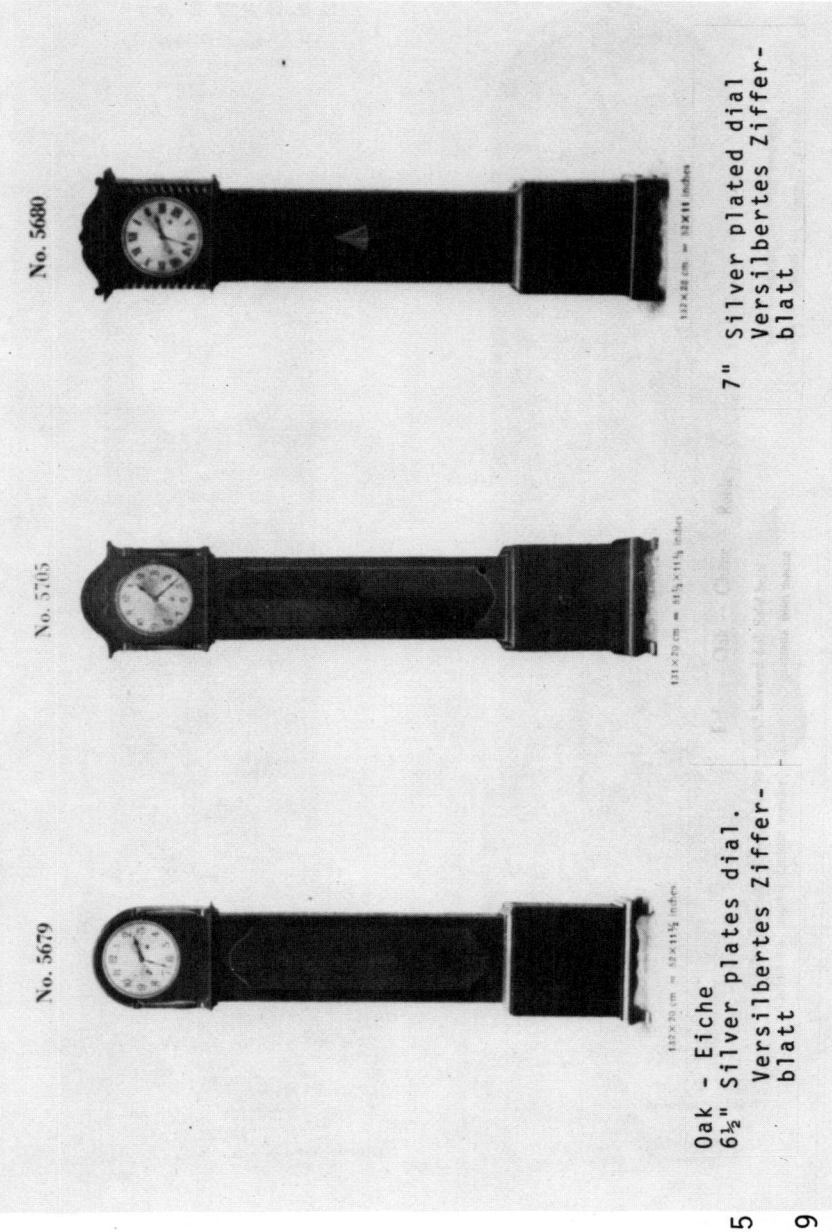

No. 5680

7" Silver plated dial
Versilbertes Ziffer-
blatt

112×28 cm = 52×11 inches

No. 5705

131×29 cm = 61½×11½ inches

No. 5679

Oak - Eiche
6½" Silver plates dial.
Versilbertes Ziffer-
blatt

132×30 cm = 52×11¾ inches

Plate 115
Cat.#D18
Year 1929

161

195 × 60 cm = 76⅝ × 23½ inches

028 186

Facetteglas – Bevelled glass
Glace à biseau – Vidrio biselado

028 187

Messingverglasung – Brass mounted glasses
Glace serties en cuivre
Cristales con engastes de latón

Eiche – Oak – Chêne – Roble
Zifferblatt – Dial – Cadran – Esfera
30 cm = 12"

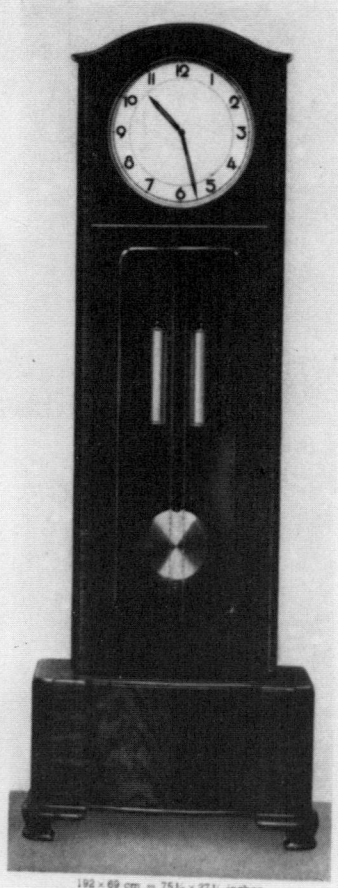

192 × 69 cm = 75½ × 27½ inches

028 205

Eiche mit Nußbaum poliert, 36 cm = 14½" Goldblatt
Oak with polished walnut, 14½" gilt dial
Chêne avec noyer poli, cadran doré, 36 cm
Roble con nogal pulido, esfera dorada, 36 cm

Plate 116
Cat.#31
Year 1930

162

Half hour-strike,base,duett,orchester or Parzifal-Gong,
or Westminster 4/4 strike system.

Nr. 5802

190 × 64 cm

Geflammt Nußbaum poliert

Facetteglas - 33 cm Zifferblatt

Flaming walnut polished
finish.
Hight= 190 cm,width 64 cm
door with bevelled glass

Nr. 5787

186 - 64 cm

Nußbaum antik - Sockelfront poliert

Facetteglas - 33 cm Mattgoldblatt - Messinggarnitur

Walnut antique-base
polished,door with
bevelled glass.
Hight= 186 cm,width
64 cm.

Plate 117
Cat.#31
Year 1930

163

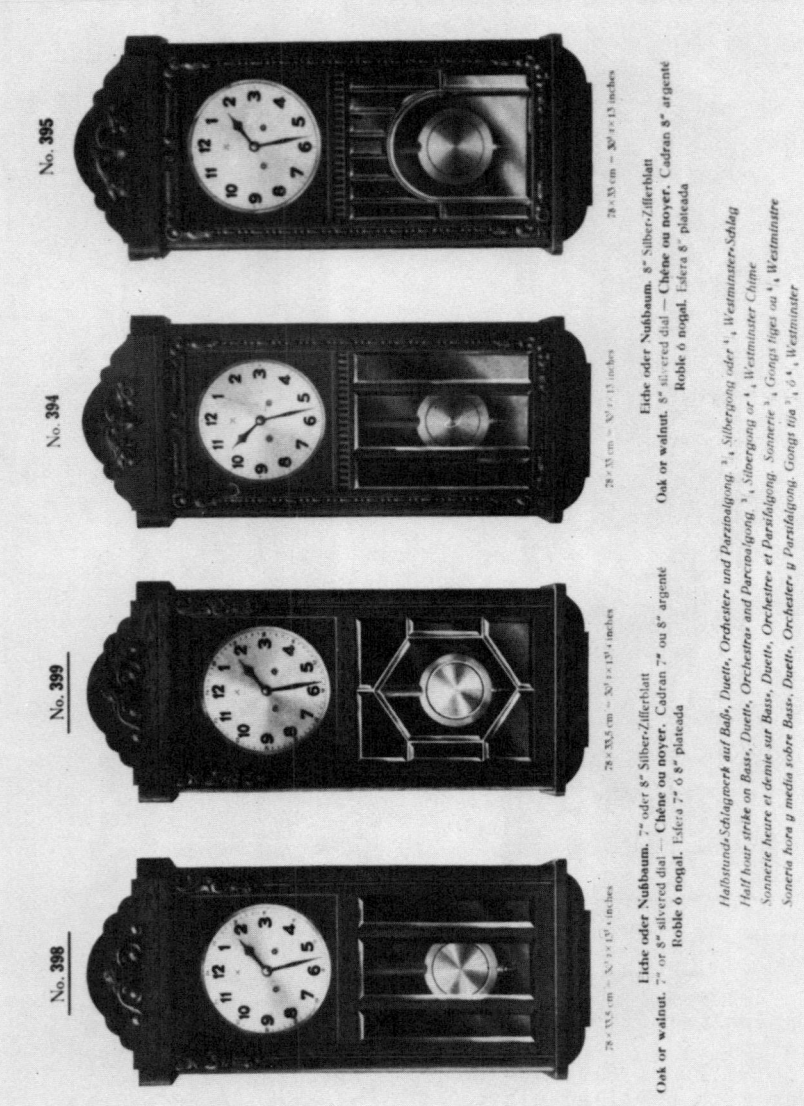

No. 398
No. 399
No. 394
No. 395

78 × 33,5 cm = 30 3/4 × 13 1/4 inches — 78 × 33,5 cm = 30 3/4 × 13 1/4 inches — 78 × 33 cm = 30 3/4 × 13 inches — 78 × 33 cm = 30 3/4 × 13 inches

Eiche oder Nußbaum. 7" oder 8" Silber-Zifferblatt
Oak or walnut. 7" or 8" silvered dial — **Chêne ou noyer.** Cadran 7" ou 8" argenté
Roble ó nogal. Esfera 7" ó 8" plateada

Eiche oder Nußbaum. 8" Silber-Zifferblatt
Oak or walnut. 8" silvered dial — **Chêne ou noyer.** Cadran 8" argenté
Roble ó nogal. Esfera 8" plateada

Halbstund-Schlagwerk auf Baß-, Duett-, Orchester- und Parzivalgong. 3/4 Silbergong oder 4/4 Westminster-Schlag
Half hour strike on Bass-, Duett-, Orchestra- and Parcivalgong. 3/4 Silbergong or 4/4 Westminster Chime
Sonnerie heure et demie sur Bass-, Duett-, Orchestre- et Parsifalgong. Sonnerie 3/4 Gongs tiges ou 4/4 Westminstre
Soneria hora y media sobre Bass-, Duett-, Orchester- y Parsifalgong. Gongs tija 3/4 ó 4/4 Westminster

Plate 118
Cat.#31
Year 1930

Half hour -strike ,base,duett,orchester or Parzifal-Gong
or Westminster-Srike system (4/4)

No. 648 No. 733 No. 751

Länge 81 cm

Länge 94 cm

Länge 80 cm

Eiche:OAK with wood
carving,ivory
color face,bevelled
glass in door.

Oak with wood
carving,walnut
or mahagony,8 1/2"
sivler plated dial.
Door with bevelled
glass.

Oak with carving
Ash,or birdmaple,
mahagony polished.
8 "silver plated
dial.
Bevelled glass with
brass decor glass
framing.

Plate 119
Cat.#31
Year 1930

165

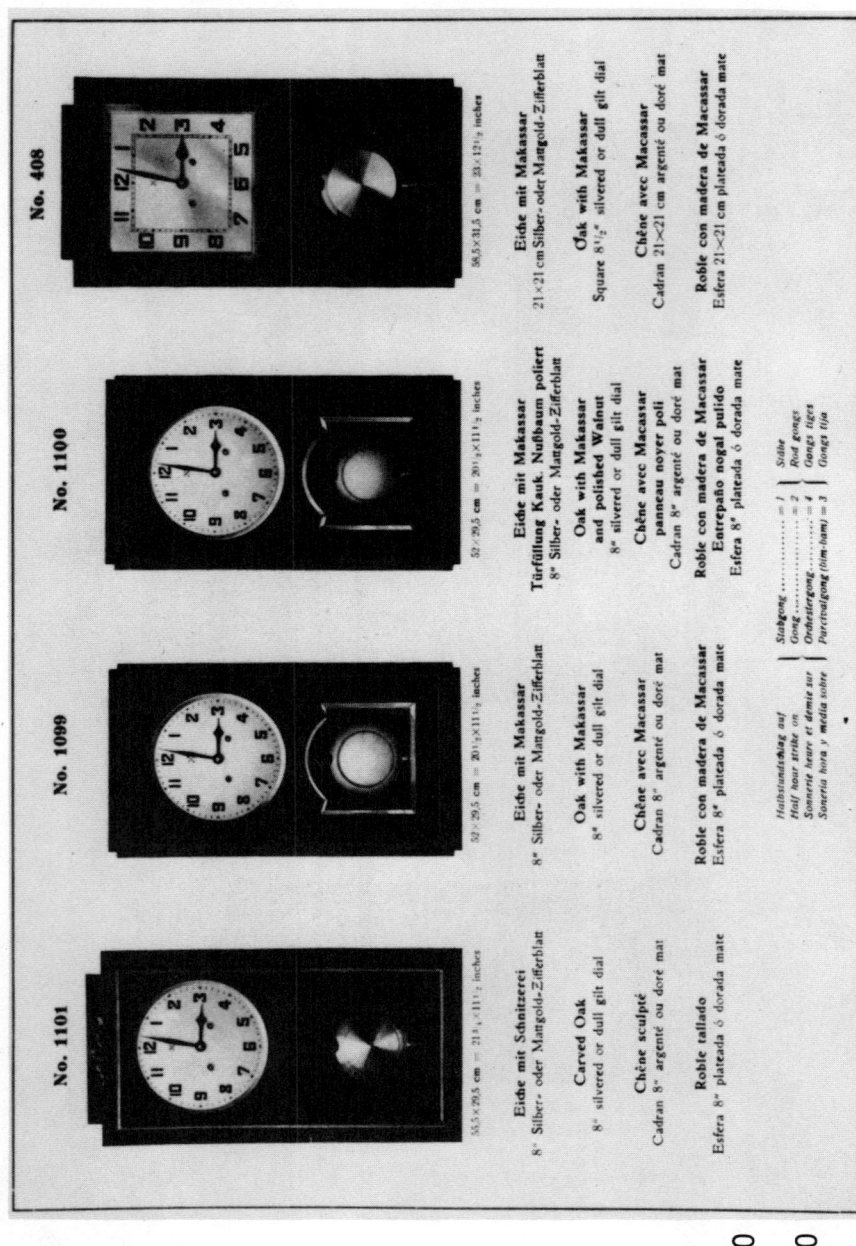

No. 1101

55,5 × 29,5 cm = 21¾ × 11½ inches

Eiche mit Schnitzerei
8" Silber- oder Mattgold-Zifferblatt

Carved Oak
8" silvered or dull gilt dial

Chêne sculpté
Cadran 8" argenté ou doré mat

Roble tallado
Esfera 8" plateada ó dorada mate

No. 1099

52 × 29,5 cm = 20½ × 11½ inches

Eiche mit Makassar
8" Silber- oder Mattgold-Zifferblatt

Oak with Makassar
8" silvered or dull gilt dial

Chêne avec Macassar
Cadran 8" argenté ou doré mat

Roble con madera de Macassar
Esfera 8" plateada ó dorada mate

No. 1100

52 × 29,5 cm = 20½ × 11½ inches

Eiche mit Makassar
Türfüllung Kauk. Nußbaum poliert
8" Silber- oder Mattgold-Zifferblatt

Oak with Makassar
and polished Walnut
8" silvered or dull gilt dial

Chêne avec Macassar
panneau noyer poli
Cadran 8" argenté ou doré mat

Roble con madera de Macassar
Entrepaño nogal pulido
Esfera 8" plateada ó dorada mate

No. 408

98,5 × 31,5 cm = 33 × 12½ inches

Eiche mit Makassar
21 × 21 cm Silber- oder Mattgold-Zifferblatt

Oak with Makassar
Square 8½" silvered or dull gilt dial

Chêne avec Macassar
Cadran 21 × 21 cm argenté ou doré mat

Roble con madera de Macassar
Esfera 21 × 21 cm plateada ó dorada mate

Halbstundschlag auf .... = 1	Stabgong
Half hour strike on .... = 2	Rod gongs
Sonnerie heure et demie sur ... = 4	Gongs tiges
Sonería hora y media sobre .... = 3	Gongs tija

Plate 120
Cat. #31
Year 1930

166

Nr. 5796   Nr. 5797   Nr. 5782 und Nr. 5783

Oak -30cm dial   Oak -33cm dial
5796=Bevelled   5782=Bevelled
      glass   glass
5797=Brass framed   5783=Brass framed
      glass   glass

Plate 123
Cat.#36
Year 1930

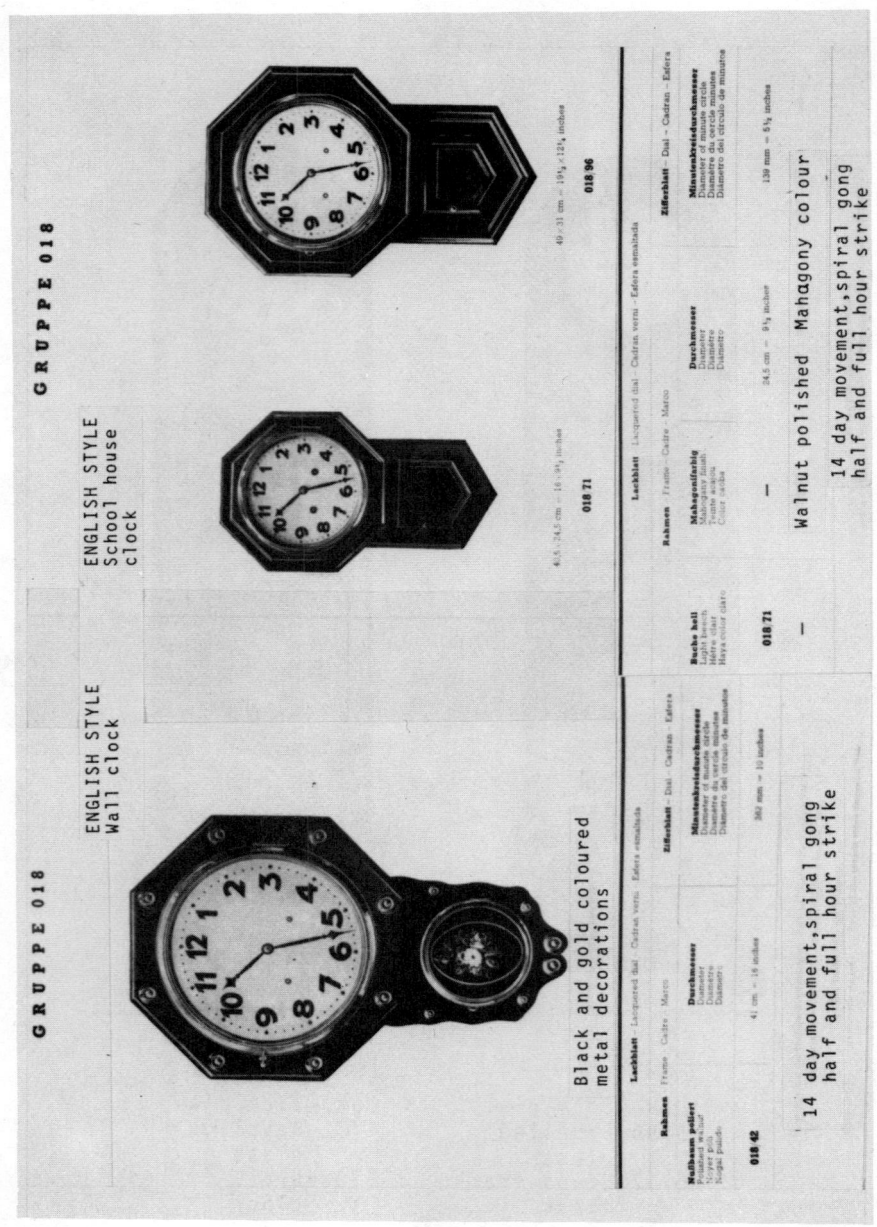

GRUPPE 018

GRUPPE 018

ENGLISH STYLE
Wall clock

ENGLISH STYLE
School house
clock

Black and gold coloured
metal decorations

Laubblatt - Lacquered dial - Cadran verni - Cadran verns - Esfera esmaltada		
Rahmen Frame · Cadre · Marco		
Nußbaum poliert Polished walnut Noyer poli Nogal pulido	**Durchmesser** Diameter Diamètre Diámetro	
018 42	41 cm = 16 inches	

Minutenkreisdurchmesser Diameter of minute circle Diamètre du cercle minutes Diámetro del círculo de minutos	
362 mm = 10 inches	

49 × 31 cm = 19¼ × 12¼ inches

018 96

Lacbblatt Lacquered dial - Cadran verni - Esfera esmaltada		
Rahmen Frame · Cadre · Marco		
Mahagonifarbig Mahogany finish Teinte acajou Color caoba	**Durchmesser** Diameter Diamètre Diámetro	

41.5 × 24.5 cm = 16 × 9¾ inches

018 71

Buche hell Light beech Hêtre clair Haya color claro	
018 71	—

24.5 cm = 9¾ inches

Zifferblatt - Dial - Cadran - Esfera	
Minutenkreisdurchmesser Diameter of minute circle Diamètre du cercle minutes Diámetro del círculo de minutos	
139 mm = 5¼ inches	

Walnut polished Mahagony colour

14 day movement,spiral gong
half and full hour strike

14 day movement,spiral gong
half and full hour strike

Plate 124
Cat.#31
Year 1930

168

Ⓒ Signature of Paul Landenberger
   Sr.petition of unified Clock
   and Watchmaker in Schramberg

Plate 125,Historical signatures
        leader of the Schram-
        berg Clock-Watchmaker.
        State Archive Stuttgart

Ⓓ Signature of Paul Landenberger
   Sr.regarding the"TRADE SCHOOL"
   in Furtwangen.
Ⓔ Signature of Arthur Junghans
   on the same document Ⓓ .
Ⓕ Signature of Paul Landenberger
   Sr."pp.Gebrüder Junghans"per
   procura,per proxy.Document to
   the Chamber of Commerce in
   Rottweil-Black Forest.

1(pg 3) Meanwhile the JUNGHANS-BROTHERS Company also was
registered as a STOCKHOLDER Corporation (A.G.).
(see page 85) The capital was owned for the most
part by the JUNGHANS family members,but was
traded on the Stock Exchange.The management remained in the hands of the JUNGHANS cousins.

2(pg 3) The fusion took place in 1932,but according to
the published catalogs the name HAMBURG-AMERICAN
Clock Company was used in 1933,1934,1935 and 1936
1937.

3(pg 3) When Helmut Junghans catered to defense contracts,
Kurt & Richard Landenberger still with the
JUNGHANS-BROTHERS A.G.until that time,did not
approved this decision and terminated at their
own request the association with JUNGHANS-BROTHERS
A.G.
Paul Landenberger,Jr.oldest son of founder PAUL
LANDENBERGER,Sr.also found the conversion of a
large portion of the production facilities for
clocks into production devices for military
defense contracts unacceptable and elected to retire early.

4(pg 4) Herr Dr.med.Fritz LANDENBERGER provided for many
years assistance to German Jews under the regime
of the -Third Reich-at great risk to his life.His
arrest would have meant confiscation of all his
property and prosecution of the members of his
family.
Herr Dr.med.Fritz LANDENBERGER negotiated with the
US Army the surrender of the City of Esslingen
avoiding further destruction and loss on lifes,an
very heroic act,since Esslingen was still surroun-
ded by German military units.

5(pg 5) The letter written to the City Council of the city
of SCHRAMBERG is proof of the many attempts undertaken by Herrn Dr.med.Fritz LANDENBERGER,to save
the Archive material of the Landenberger family
for future generations.The author has heard that
the city of Schramberg in 1978 began the process
of providing a location for the Landenberger
Archive,to be called the "LANDENBERGER MEMORIAL
ROOM"

6(pg 6) Since then the late Dr.med.Fritz Landenberger's
will has been probated and executed,placing a very
large amount of money in trust for the Landenberger
Memorial Room.

7(pg 8) For historical accuracy the original presentation
of the contents of the FIFTIETH ANNIVERSARY of
the HAMBURG AMERICAN Clock Company has been faith-
fully reproduced only in reduced format.

cont.CHAPTER XXVIII

8(pg 11) See location map (page 80,Table II).

9(pg 13) See location map (page 80,Table II).

10(pg 33) R.NÄGELE,graphic artist,did much works for the
HAU *(HAMBURG-AMERICAN-UHRENFABRIK)*.As a victim
of the -Third Reich-laws*(The Nurenberger Laws)*,
Nägele was part Jewish,he was not allowed to practice graphic art after 1933.Nägele emigrated to
the USA,returning to his beloved "Black Forest"
after 1945.There he died several years later(exact
date unknown).He was laid to rest near Freiburg
*(see location map page 80)*in the Black Forest.
His graphics are exhibited in the Guggenheimer
Museum (New York),his creative art work now classified internationally as very valuable.

11(pg 46)See page 30,plates 29 and 30.

12(pg 64)The daughter and Granddaughter of Herrn Victor
LUSCHKA are now living in Schramberg.Ms.Susanne
Luschka an elementary school teacher,takes care
of her aged mother in their home on the Luschka
estate in Schramberg.

13(pg 75)Paul Landenberger,Sr.maintained a close realation-
ship with all his working poeple,his "Old timers"
sending personal notes to all his workers he never
let a holiday-birthday pass without them.

14(pg 77)After writing controversial letter about "Herrn
Schmid"*(Woodshop superindentend of HAU)*Herr Paul
Landenberger,Sr.changed his mind and provided a
good deal of efforts and considerable support for
a"TECHNICAL SCHOOL"in Furtwangen.The School was
then subsequently founded and is still in existence
with an outstanding reputation."DIE UHRENMACHER
des HOHEN SCHWARZWALD"*(in GERMAN the CLOCKMAKER
of the HIGH BLACK FOREST)*a reference to GERD BENDER
-the author-a teacher in this School.An artist
rendering of the TRADE SCHOOL in Furtwangen can be
seen on page 211 of "THE BLACK FOREST CUCKOO CLOCK"
1979 edition by Karl Kochmann.

15(pg 82)From the Archive of the Library of Science,London,
England:*"WARENZEICHENBLATT"issued by the Emperors
German Patent Office,BERLIN"*

16(pg 86)From the personal file of fellow clock collector
Harvey Silk,CPT USAF,Heidelberg,Germany.

17(pg 176)Meeting the anticipated target date for and holding
the pricetag on this publication down were hampered
with immense difficulties due the ever-mounting
cost for labor and materials.

1(Seite 24) Gebrüder JUNGHANS war zwischenzeitlich eben-
falls eine Aktiengesellschaft geworden,deren
Kapital zum Teil im Besitze der Familien
Junghans,zum grösseren Teil aber an der Börse
gehandelt wurde.Die Firma wurde von den
Junghans Vettern geleitet.

2(Seite 25) Die Fusion kam zustande,bis schließlich-ent-
gegen des Fusionsvertrages-der Firmenname des
"Kleineren Partners"verschwand.*(Anmerkung des
Authors)*Kataloge als Archivmaterial für diese
Publication beginnend mit dem Jahre 1933,1934,
1934,1936 und 1937,der Name HAMBURG-AMERIKANISCHE
UHRENFABRIK wurde von Junghans verwendet.

3(Seite 25) .....einer unpersönlichen Arbeit wich.Besonders
schmerzlich war für die alten HAU-Mitarbeiter,
daß Helmut Junghans 1936 ins Rüstungsgeschäft
einstieg,was die Brüder Kurt und Richard
Landenberger veranlaßte aus der Firma auszu -
scheiden.Paul Landenberger der Jüngere-der
älteste Sohn des Firmengründers der HAU,ging
vorzeitig in Pension.

4(Seite 28) Herr Dr.med Fritz Landenberger hat unter dem
Einsatz seines Lebens,und großer Gefahr für
seine Familie und Besitz für viele Jahre Deutsche
Juden beschützt und für sie gesorgt.

5(Seite 28) Dieses Schreiben an die Stadtverwaltung-Bürger-
meister-in Schramberg zeigt das tiefe Interesse
das Herr Dr.med.Fritz Landenberger hatte,um die
Archiv-Bestände der Landenberger Familie vor dem
Verlust zu retten.Nach seinem Tode im Jahre 1978
hat die Erbschaftsverwaltung sich mit der Stadt
Schramberg ins Benehmen gesetzt.

6(Seite 30) Aus der Erbnachlassenschaft wurde ein sehr großer
Betrag für die"LANDENBERGER GEDÄCHNIS STIFTUNG"
abgezweigt.

7(Seite 32) Aus historischen Gründen wurde der gesamte Inhalt
der"DENKSCHRIFT zum 50 jährigen Bestehen der
HAMBURG-AMERIKANISCHEN UHRENFABRIK"als geschlo-
ssener Nachdruck wiedergegeben.

8(Seite 36) Siehe Orientierungskarte Seite 80,Tafel II
9(Seite 40) Siehe Orientierungskarte Seite 80,Tafel II
10(Seite 33) R.NÄGELE,als freiberuflicher Graphiker,war für
viele Jahre für HAU tätig.Nach 1933 war es Nägele
nicht erlaubt seinen Beruf weiterhin auszuüben,
nachdem er auf Grund der*"Nürnberger Gesetze"*
als Halbjude nicht als Mitglied der Kulturkammer
zugelassen wurde.Er verließ Deutschland,machte
sich in den USA seßhaft,kehrte nach 1945 wieder
in den Schwarzwald zurück.Er starb dort und ist
in der Nähe von Freiburg beerdigt.Seine graphischen
Arbeiten sind heute anerkannte künstlerische Werke
und sind im Guggenheimer Museum-New York oft aus-
stellt worden.Sie sind unter Sammlern als Wert-
volle Kunstobjekte begehrt.

11(Seite 46)Siehe Seite 30,Abbildung 29 und 30.

12(Seite 64)Fräulein Susanne Luschka(Enkeltoschter) des
Herrn Victor LUSCHKA,lebt mit ihrer Mutter
Frau Luschka,Ehefrau des Herrn Victor Luschka
jun.+ 1978(siehe Seite 78)in Schramberg.

13(Seite 75)Nach Aussagen einiger Bürger in Schramberg und
aus dem Archivmaterial kann man ersehen,daß Herr
Paul Landenberger sen.immer ein großes Interesse
an dem Wohlergehen und der Wohlfahrt seiner
(ALLER)Mitarbeiter hatte.Eine Fürsorgekasse(Die
Hauptbücher)sind noch erhalten beweisen daß die
Landenberger Familie aus einem persönlichen Etat
große Beträge für eine Unterstützungskasse zur
Verfügung stellte,um in Härtefällen den Betroffe-
nen auszuhelfen.

14(Seite 77)Dieses Schreiben,mit dem Briefkopf der Firma
*"LANDENBERGER & LANG"*wurde später mit anderen
Schreiben durch Herrn Landenberger sen.überholt.
Er hat sich darin sehr für die von Herrn"Schmid"
empfohlene Fachschule in Furtwangen eingesetzt.
Die Fachschule besteht heute noch und erfreut
sich eines ausgezeichneten Rufes.

15(Seite 82)Mit freundlicher Genehmigung in der Orginalgröße
von der Biblothek für Forschung in LONDON-England
ein Auszug aus dem*"WARENZEICHENBLATT des*
KAISERLICHEN PATENTAMTES in
BERLIN.Jahrgang 1901"

16(Seite 86)Mit freundlicher Genehmigung aus dem Archiv
Uhrensammler Kollege Mr.Harvey Silk Heidelberg
(BRD)

17(Seite
176)   Viele Schwierigkeiten,besonders durch die
ständigen Preissteigerungen im Druckgewerbe her-
vorgerufen,haben die Herausgabe der HAU Schrift
sehr behindert.

TABLE of CONTENTS
INHALTSVERZEICHNIS

NOTES: + Abbreviation for HAMBURG-AMERICAN
                      CLOCK Co.
*(German)** Partially with english sub titles

174

Research work
"After work"
in the
"PARADISE INN"
Schramberg

Plate 126

Dear Reader:

In the 1978 edition of *THE BLACK FOREST CUCKOO CLOCK* I promised readers
I would publish two additional histories, *THE HAMBURG AMERICAN CLOCK CO.* and a
combined volume on the Lenzkirch and the Winterhalder clock companies. But the
urgent need to reprint the *TRADEMARK INDEX* delayed my publication program. For
several months a concentrated effort to produce the expanded, greatly revised
1980 edition of the *INDEX* required all my personal "leisure time." After successfully completing that major effort, I intended to take a rest. I thought
my one-man publishing company's tape recorder, pen, and typewriter should
accumulate a little dust.

But it was not possible. Too many readers from all over the world wrote
to compliment my previous writings on industrialized European clockmaking.
These letters provided great encouragement for pursuing my one-man project. My
circle of friends turned out to be widely enlarged, especially in England. On
my last visit in 1979 I found I was no longer a stranger. The chap from
California who writes on Black Forest cultural-technical history was very well
received--I was amongst a lot of friends.

In the past years I have spent a lot of time on the subject of horology.
I provide information for the collector of European clocks of the industrialized
era. Many letters expressed a feeling that the only clocks available to most
collectors were those industrially produced; those from an earlier age, the top
museum timepieces, were inaccessible to many friends of old clocks.

175

The reader will notice the absence in this volume of my customary
Collector's Gallery, which pictured a variety of HAU clocks. No Historical
Pricelist is reproduced either. I have noticed that various "Collector's" clocks
shown in previous publications have subsequently been used as commercial
vehicles, their prices jolted sky-high. My intention is to provide a source of
historical-educational information, not a sales catalog.

Often I am told, "You must make a lot of money!" Let me assure you, I
am happy if I cover all expenses. I am not a publisher in the sense of a publishing house, but rather very private--for me it is more than a business. With
all these thoughts in mind, I opened the *HAMBURG AMERICAN CLOCK CO.* file again
and began the sixth book in my series on European industrialized clockmaking.
I hope to continue to be of assistance to the collector, the hobbyist, the
historian, and those who are simply interested in the subject of mass-produced
clockmaking. Their continued faithful support of my publications is very much
appreciated.

A collector writing for collectors,

Karl Kochmann

September 1980   KARL KOCHMANN

ACKNOWLEDGMENTS

Special thanks to Herrn WalterFlaig,Stuttgart,West
Germany,for his outstanding support and his laison work
in arranging all correspondence with and my visit to his
late granduncle by marriage,Herrn Dr.med.F.Landenberger
.....To the JUNGHANS Company,Schramberg,for allowing one
time access(1975)to the stored archive of HAU,located
within the former property of the HAU Company.Research
support(1977)was witheld,............................
    Herrn Johannes Hennig,Horologist,Lecturer,Master
Watchmaker in Dresden GDR(East Germany),for his research
assistance on the project.....
    To the Stammelbach family in Schramberg,owners of the
traditional "INN of PARADISE",who made my stay so pleasant
    while I was researching the *HAMBURG-AMERICAN CLOCK
Company*,and the Msd.Susanne Luschka,for additional archive
material,for their hospitality,which made research work in
Schramberg economically possible.....
    To Cheryl Kent,whose editing,proofreading,and typing
scills were of great assistance in preparing the final
manuscript for publication......
    To the horological booksellers and clock material
supply houses for their supportive efforts to market my
publications worldwide,for otherwise these limited
editions could not be made aviable to subscribers from
organized clock collectors' clubs at a reasonable price,
.....
    To Merrill Parker,photographer,for his dedicated
efforts to provide all photographic art work for this
publication........
    And,finally,for all her administrative help an the
never-ending trouble she takes to fill all special
requests,my wife Ingrid deserves a grateful thank you.

****

Besonderen Dank Herrn Walter Flaig,Stuttgart,für
seine Mitarbeit..............
......JUNGHANS-DIEHL Uhrenfabrik in Schramberg,
erlaubte eine einmalige Einsicht in das Archiv-
material im Jahre 1975,weitere Nachforschungen
(Jahr 1977)wurden nicht ermöglicht.............
......Herrn Johannes Hennig,Dresden,DDR,Uhrmacher-
meister,Lektor und Sammler-Kollege für seine selbst-
lose Mithilfe...............
......Für die gastfreundliche Aufnahme im Gasthof
"ZUM PARADIES".Dank der Stammelbach Familie,und den
Damen Luschka,für ihre Unterstützung während meines
Aufenthaltes in Schramberg........................
......Ms.Cheryl Kent,San Franzisko,Kalifornien,für
die gesamte Bearbeitung des Englischen Textes......
......Merrill Parker,Concord,Kalifornien,für seine
photographische Mitarbeit sei bestens gedankt.

******

Der Verfasser